"[Brown] probably knows more about cows than Faulkner knew about mules, which is saying something."
—Jonathan Yardley, *The Washington Post*

"Larry Brown . . . is one of the best there is. . . . By cultivating awe of the ordinary, Brown exhibits an extraordinary talent."
—L. Elisabeth Beattle, *Lexington Herald-Leader*

"Unromantic, unembellished, full of humor, honesty, and wisdom, the essays themselves are the stories of a man bound to the land on which he lives."
—Julie Hale, *Bookpage*

"Brown's muscular sentences hold us in the intensity of the moment, combining forceful description with unexpected tenderness."
—Tommy Hays, *The Atlanta Journal-Constitution*

"Often startling . . . unique and highly readable."
—*Booklist*

"Geography and truth. Brown threads them together in prose so quiet and so direct that it's too easy to miss the art that hides the art."
—William Starr, *The Star Reporter* (Columbia, S.C.)

LARRY BROWN

BILLY RAY'S FARM

ESSAYS

TOUCHSTONE
PUBLISHED BY SIMON & SCHUSTER
NEW YORK   LONDON   TORONTO
SYDNEY   SINGAPORE

Touchstone
Rockefeller Center
1230 Avenue of the Americas
New York, NY 10020

First Touchstone Edition 2002

Published by arrangement with Algonquin Books of Chapel Hill

TOUCHSTONE and colophon are registered trademarks
of Simon & Schuster, Inc.

For information about special discounts for bulk purchases,
please contact Simon & Schuster Special Sales at 1-800-456-6798
or business@simonandschuster.com

Manufactured in the United States of America
1 3 5 7 9 10 8 6 4 2

The Library of Congress has cataloged the Algonquin Books
edition as follows:
Brown, Larry.
Billy Ray's farm / by Larry Brown.
p.   cm.
"A Shannon Ravenel book."
1. Brown, Larry, 1951 July 9—Homes and haunts—
Mississippi—Oxford Region. 2. Oxford Region (Miss.)—Social
life and customs. 3. Novelists, American—20th century—
Biography. 4. Fathers and sons—Mississippi—Oxford Region.
5. Farm life—Mississippi—Oxford Region. I. Title.
PS3552.R6927Z466   2001
813'.54—dc21   [B]   00-067536

ISBN 1-56512-167-8
0-7432-2524-4 (Pbk)

This book, naturally,
is for Billy Ray.

GRATEFUL ACKNOWLEDGMENT is made for the original publication of the following essays, some of which appear here with a few changes: "By the Pond," *Glamour*; "Thicker than Blood," *Outside*; "Harry Crews: Mentor and Friend," *The Southern Quarterly*; "Chattanooga Nights," *The Chattahoochee Review*; "Billy Ray's Farm," *The Oxford American*; "Fishing with Charlie," *The Oxford American*; "So Much Fish, So Close to Home: An Improv," *The Chattahoochee Review*; "The Whore in Me," AOL, *The Book Report*; and "Goatsongs," *Men's Journal*.

CONTENTS

BILLY RAY'S FARM

PROLOGUE

A LONG TIME AGO when I was a boy, there was one slab of concrete that stretched from Oxford to Toccopola, a distance of about sixteen miles, and that was the road everybody used to get to town. It was kind of like half of a road, with one side concrete, the other side dirt and gravel. If you were heading *to* town, you could stay on the concrete all the way and never have to get off on the gravel side. And if you were coming *from* town, you could get on the concrete part and drive on the wrong side of the road until you met somebody, and then you had to jump back onto the gravel.

That road has been gone for a long time, but I still remember the swaying of the car as my father went from one side of the road to the other. Everybody did it and nobody ever thought anything about it.

A trip to town on Saturday was a big event. The Square in Oxford has changed some, true, but by and large it still retains the image I have of it from thirty years ago. It is still lined with stores and parked cars, and the big oaks still stand on the courthouse lawn, and the Confederate soldier is still standing there high above everything so that you can see him first when you come up the long drive of South Lamar. What has changed is the nature of the town. A long time ago you could find people selling vegetables from the backs of their trucks, and you could go in Winter's Cafe and get a hamburger and a short-bottled Coke for sixty-five cents. You can't even buy an Egg McMuffin on University Avenue for that.

Faulkner would probably be flabbergasted to know that there are several bars on the Square now, and that blues music can often be heard wailing out of the open doors on hot summer nights, floating around the air on the Square, lifting up to the balconies of the apartments that line the south side, where people are having drinks and conversing. It's not like it was when he was around. Life was hard for some. Blacks were oppressed. The drinking fountains on the Square were labeled Colored and White. That world doesn't exist anymore.

What does exist is the memory of it, a faded remnant of the way things were. Write about what you know, yes, even if it doesn't exist anymore.

When I wrote my novel *Father and Son*, people wondered why I set it back in the sixties. The answer to that is very simple. When I wrote the first scene, where Glen Davis and his brother Puppy are driving back into town, I didn't see the Square I see now, with Square Books on the left side of South Lamar and Proud Larrys' on the right. I saw that old Oxford, the one where Grace

Crockett's shoe store stood in the place now occupied by a restaurant and bar called City Grocery, and I saw the old trucks with wooden roofs built over the back ends to shield the watermelons and roasting ears and purple hull peas from the heat of the sun, and I saw a battered old dusty car that my two characters were riding in, and I knew that it had a shift on the column, and an AM radio with push buttons, and musty upholstery that had once been velvet. I saw all that and I knew that they had driven in one hot Saturday afternoon back during my childhood, and I remember the way things were.

What is it about Oxford that produces writers? I get asked that question a lot, and so does Barry Hannah, and so does John Grisham, and I have to confess that I'm just as bewildered by that question as the people who continue to ask it. Maybe even more so. They always want to ask about Faulkner and *what it all means*, being a writer in Oxford, and where all the stories come from, and why that environment seems to nurture writers. No matter where I go, I always get hit with that question or a variation of it.

I don't know what the answer is for anybody else, and I don't know what caused Faulkner to write. Most times, for any writer, I think it springs from some sort of yearning in the breast to let things out, to say something about the human condition, maybe just to simply tell a story. When pressed really hard, I say something generic like, "Well, for me the land sort of creates the *characters*, you know? I mean I look at the people around me and wonder what their stories are, or I think of some character and put him in a situation and then follow him around for a while, see what happens next."

It's hard sometimes while being pressed into a corner of the wallpaper to come up with a satisfying answer about your own land and the influences it has on you. Most of this stuff is private. You could say that you like the way the sky looks just before a big thunderstorm moves across a river bottom, or that you like to see the thousands of tiny frogs that emerge on the roads on a balmy spring night just after a good shower. You could ruminate expansively about the beauty of a hardwood forest on a cold morning, or the way the distant trees stand shimmering against the horizon on a blistering summer day. But none of that would satisfy the question. What is it they really want to know? Probably nothing more than that old and tired favorite: *Where do you get your ideas?*

I believe that writers have to write what they know about. I don't think there's much choice in that. The world Faulkner wrote about was vastly different from the one that exists now. If Faulkner were alive today, he would see that. The mansion down the street has been replaced by a BP gas station now, and the hardwood forest the dogs once yammered through has been clear-cut and turned into a pine plantation. Black folks don't say "yassuh" any more, and at this moment I would have no idea where in all of Lafayette County I could find a good mule. I think the past influenced Faulkner a lot. It must have, since so many of his stories and novels are about segments of history that had already passed when he wrote of them. All he was doing was what every other writer does, and that is drawing upon the well of memory and experience and imagination that every writer pulls his or her material from. The things you know, the things you have seen or heard of, the things you can imagine. A writer rolls all that stuff together kind of like a taco and comes up with fiction. And I think whatever you write about, you have to know it. Concretely. Absolutely. Realistically.

Oxford produces writers for the same reason that New York does, or Knoxville, or Milledgeville, or Bangor. You can't pick where you're born or raised. You take what you're given, whether it's the cornfields of the Midwest or the coal mines of West Virginia, and you make your fiction out of it. It's all you have. And somehow, wherever you are, it always seems to be enough.

By the Pond

THE BOAT DOCK juts out over a little cove that's sheltered by a leaning cedar tree, one of the few that survived the ice storm last February, and if I could have picked one tree to save, it would have been that one. It shades the dock and sheds its needles onto the planks, and the bullfrogs I released this spring pick that spot to sit, where it's cool.

I bought the place five or six years ago, but I fished in the pond when I was a boy. There's a pasture in front and a small barn on the hill. The tin on the barn's roof is rusted to a nice even brown, and it's pretty old, but it still keeps the rain out.

The back side of the pond is mostly woods, really big pines and a few oaks that form a deep and compelling sanctuary for the birds and the rabbits and one lone armadillo. When the water is still, the trees surrounding the pond are reflected on the surface in a perfect reverse image of willow and gum and poplar. Some of the smaller pines got snapped off in the storm, but the big ones are okay.

The place is only eight acres, and it looked bad when I got it. It was overgrown with what I called briar bushes, black-tipped thorn vines that cut my skin like a razor and stung like fire. I spent the first summer clearing it, cutting the matted tangles and piling them to burn later. I would work until my clothes were dripping with sweat, until my eyes were nearly blinded with it and I was too tired to keep on, then I'd drive home with that good feeling of having done a day's work and come back and do it again the next morning. It was hard labor, but I didn't mind. It made me sleep well at night.

The pond was worse. It was old, too, and at one time it was full of bass, but a pond will decline over the years. It needed cleaning out and restocking. There were downed trees in it, and I had to wade in there with my chain saw and cut them up, slinging water and mud, then back my little truck down to the edge of the water and pull them out with a log chain. I piled up the trees and waited for them to dry, and on cold fall days I burned them in great leaping fires that lasted into the night.

I wanted a boat dock, so three summers ago I pumped the water down far enough to dry out the cove, and I hired some boys who owned a bulldozer. I worked in the bottom of the pond for eleven straight days, digging holes and setting the posts in concrete, stringing timbers and nailing the frame together, trying to keep it all level while the others dozed dirt and carved away at the old banks, making the pond longer, wider, deeper. When I nailed on the planks for the walkway and the deck, the pond was ready for some rain, and then finally, some fish.

One cold November afternoon in Oxford, Mary Annie and Shane stood with me in a stiff wind beside a hatchery truck from Oklahoma and waited while a tall cowboy dipped out tiny black crappie, channel catfish, and a hundred Florida bass into plastic bags full of ice-cold water. We made a fast run out to the pond, knelt on the boat dock and lowered them into the water, and watched as the little fish swam out into the dark depths, vanishing into their world. It felt good to do that, to see new life heading out to explore and grow.

My friends from town come out in warm weather to fish or camp out and they bring their children, Tom with Julian and Glennray with Zack. I like to see little boys fishing, learning this sport of patience and discovering the beauty of nature's gifts. Sometimes Randy or Charlie or Rick will come out and fish with me, drifting in the boat and lazing away an afternoon, and it's one of those rare things that's peaceful and good for your soul.

I lived almost ten years of my early life beside a railroad track in Memphis, and I never stopped longing to

live in Mississippi, where I was born, and to be in the
country, a place like this. Maybe it was the big engines
that rolled the length of the Southern Avenue rails day
and night, always going somewhere with their sad and
thunderous air horns and their endless lines of freight
cars, that gave me the feeling of being trapped somehow within the city. Maybe it was all the little houses
stacked tightly side by side behind their tiny yards, or
just the simple desire a boy has for a dog, a place to fish,
a place to roam. Whatever it was, I knew I'd never be
happy there. It's one thing to have a life in a place, and
to be happy in it is quite another.

Now, in fall once again, the water along the shallow
edges is the color of tea, and schools of small fish dart
out from the timbers when I step onto the boat dock,
and the sweet gums are turning red and orange and
dropping their leaves onto the glassy surface. The frogs
and snakes are deep in their mud by now, and their
blood will stay chilled until spring comes again and the
warm winds blow. I sit and watch the water, and look at
the ice-shattered pines, and think of all the work I still
have to do, with chain saw and sweat, in July's burning
air. But for now I can just rest in the ragged lawn chair
and see the occasional splash of a feeding yearling bass.
No matter what else is going wrong, I can feel better by
just sitting for a while, as the leaves keep wafting down,
as the wind rustles the grass and moves the water. I may

not ever own much else in my life, but this is enough. Or almost enough. One of these days when I get through cleaning up from the storm, I'm going to start building a little cabin right over there above the pond, up in the deep part of that shade.

Thicker than Blood

TWO YEARS BEFORE my father died, when I was fourteen, my great-uncle Dave Hallman gave me a 12-gauge single-barrel shotgun that was rusted to a smooth brown, the stock patched together and full of dents and scratches. The yellow veins of glue still show where it rests in my gun cabinet today. It would blow open with the shot because the breech lock was so worn, but it was what I had and I used it gladly. To be able to take that ancient piece that had already been in so many other hands and go out into the fall woods and sit against a hickory tree and kill two or three squirrels of an evening after school and take them home just past dark and skin them for my mother's black-iron skillet was a fine thing for a boy to be able to do.

Daddy didn't hunt, didn't even own a gun, although he took me fishing plenty of times. Hunting was just something he didn't do, and I suspect that four years of fighting in World War II might have had something to do with it, all the killing of men with guns he'd seen. It was left to other people to take me to the Mississippi woods and show me the ways of them.

There was Uncle Ont, who had chickens in the yard of his big old house, and herds of cows and goats and dogs. The dogs were hounds, and they were all sizes, all breeds, Bluetick or Redbone mixed in with Black and Tan or Treeing Walker to sometimes produce enormous coondogs with specks or spots and bugle throats and big feet and long ears. He gave them names like Lisa and Nimrod and Naman. We drove to the river bottoms and cornfields in open pickups filled with baying hounds. Sometimes we hunted almost all night, and Mother never failed to roll me out for school the next morning.

Robert Fulton Jones was named for the man who invented the steamboat but everybody we knew called him Sam. He showed me secret, primo squirrel woods and we drove to them in a 1958 Impala, two-tone blue, guns on the backseat, tobacco juice out the window. We combed the edges of creek-bottom fields with his lemon pointer and flushed coveys of birds while the shotguns spoke on cold January afternoons. I took thirty days' leave from the marines in the fall of 1971 and hunted squirrels every day I was home. Sam was still alive then and he lived to see my own sons as little boys with fishing poles in their hands. Mr. Sam, they called him, just like I did.

I was lucky to spend my teenage years in a little community called Tula. There were only about a hundred and fifty people there. We had a store, two churches. There had been a college there many years ago and there was still a high school there until 1963. Most of the roads were gravel and back in those days, with the energy and strength of a young man's legs, I could walk to plenty of places to hunt.

My brother Knox had a beautiful hound named Sheila. She had a great yodel voice that quavered when she was trailing and all I had to do was get her on the leash and find my flashlight and boots and walk out of the front yard into the black woods and down to the Yocona River bottom, the big wild one with leaf-strewn sloughs and fresh beaver dams. The tall cypresses with their knees in standing water were hollow coon castles, the bark worn smooth on one side only from the steady traffic of coons scrambling up in the morning and down at night, regular as dairymen.

One day my newly married friend, Harold Keel, and I were poking around down there and climbed a hollow snag to look quietly into a den and see masked babies mewling and sucking at the fat gray nipples of their sleeping mother, a small nest of intense life in the drowsing summer woods, safe from us on that day. Those times seem like dreams now. But I was just a boy.

I don't think the older men who let me hunt with

them ever put their heads together after my father died suddenly in 1968 and came up with a plan to educate me in the fine points of guns and dogs. They knew my parents because they had all grown up together, and it just happened naturally in that little place, me going with them.

They're all dead and gone, have been for years. I can walk in the cemetery in Tula and see their headstones, stand and read their names now chiseled in granite, marble. I think often of the great gift they gave me—this common act of sharing their hounds and their carbide lanterns and their secret places to hunt—which in its many forms boiled down to just one thing: their time. Maybe in some unspoken way they took care of me because of us losing Daddy so early. Probably I would have hunted with them even if he'd lived. But in the reserves of good memories we all hold, those times are special and seem magical to me, those nights in the woods and those days in the fields, those lessons in the wild.

My boys' guns are beside mine in the cabinet now, next to the old one Uncle Dave gave me. They bring in ducks and squirrels and deer and doves, and I cook for them as my mother did for me, and they tell me their hunting stories, and I listen to catch their words.

Harry Crews: Mentor and Friend

I'VE BEEN READING Harry Crews for so long that I can't really remember when I first discovered his work. It was probably way back in some dim year close to the time when I started writing, and that was in 1980. I remember that my friend and cousin, Paul Hipp, came over one afternoon when my wife and children and I were living in the house with my mother-in-law. He had in his hand a paperback copy of *A Feast of Snakes,* and he loaned it to me. I can remember sitting on the front porch in the swing, reading it. My children were small then, Billy Ray only three or four, Shane just a baby, LeAnne not even born yet. I remember how that book moved me, shook me, riveted me. I'd never read anything like it and didn't know that such things could be done in a book. I didn't know that a man could invent characters like Joe Lon Mackey, or his sister, Beeder, or Buddy Matlow, the peg-legged sheriff. It was a combination of hilarity and stark reality and beauty and sadness. Since then I've read it many times, and like all great books, it only gets better with each reading.

I'd already seen some of his essays in places like *Playboy* and *Esquire*, and somewhere along in there I went to Richard Howorth's fledgling bookstore in Oxford and bought a book of essays called *Florida Frenzy*. From the library I checked out a book called *Blood and Grits*, and another one called *A Childhood: The Biography of a Place*. I was awed by his writing, by the stories of his life, his childhood, his struggles to become a writer, the places he had been and the things he had done. His novels were harder to find. The public library had a couple of them, *The Gypsy's Curse* and *The Hawk Is Dying*. I read both of those and loved them, but I couldn't find any more of his fiction. I knew it was out there somewhere, but nobody seemed to know where.

I don't know how long a period of time this reading covered, but I was trying to write by then. I was in the process of trying to find mentors, writers whose work I could look up to and gain inspiration from. I wanted to read the rest of those books, novels that were listed in the front pages of his other books, novels with names like *Karate Is a Thing of the Spirit*, *Naked in Garden Hills*, *This Thing Don't Lead to Heaven*, *Car*, *The Gospel Singer*.

I went in search of a larger library, and found it out at Ole Miss. I learned all over again how to use the card catalog, and then, armed with a piece of paper I had scribbled letters and numbers on, I began to prowl the stacks. And I began to find the books. Most of them were there, minus their dust jackets, and I checked them out and took them home and read them. *Car* was released in paperback and I bought it, and when *The Gospel Singer* was finally released again in 1988, I bought it. As the newer books have come out, things like *The Knockout Artist* and *All We Need of Hell* and *Body* and *Scar Lover* and *The Mulching of America*, I've bought them. I've read or bought everything by him that I've been able to get my hands on, and I'm grateful that a writer like him walks this earth.

By 1985 I HAD written five unpublished novels and almost one hundred short stories that had, for the most part, gone begging also. I'd sold one story to *Easyriders*, one to *Fiction International*, and one to a now-defunct magazine in New York called *Twilight Zone*. I had learned by then that the price of success for a writer came high, that there were years of a thing called the apprenticeship period, and that nobody could tell you when you'd come to the end of it. You just had to keep writing with blind faith, and hope, and trust in yourself that you would eventually find your way, that the world would one day accept your work.

Whenever I fell into a black period of depression,

which was fairly often, I could get one of Harry's books of essays and read again about what he had gone through, how he had worked for years with no success. It was comforting somehow to know that a man of his great talent had not been born to it, but had learned it, and had possessed the perseverance or stubbornness or internal character or whatever it was that he possessed that allowed him to keep on writing in the face of rejection. I read about how much he had lost: his family, one of his boys. He never once complained about how tough it had been. He never said how hard it was to put the words down. What he said was that you had to keep your ass in the chair. Even if he couldn't write anything one day, if it wouldn't come at that particular sitting, he would make himself sit in the chair for three hours anyway. I knew that back in those days when he was unpublished, he must have wanted success as badly as I did then. And I was tremendously heartened to read these things. It meant that I was not the only person who had ever gone through what I was enduring, that it was probably a universal experience, this apprenticeship period, this time when you wrote things that were not good only to throw them away or have them rejected in order to write enough to eventually learn how.

I burned one of my novels in the backyard. I collected my rejection slips and kept them in a worn manila envelope. I kept writing, and hoping, and trying to do better. I pulled a twenty-four-hour shift at the fire department in Oxford ten days a month, and on the other days I drove nails or sacked groceries or cleaned carpets, whatever it took to make a few extra dollars to feed my growing family, heat the house, pay the bills that everybody has. On the weekends or for a few hours at night I would go into the kitchen and try to write something that made some sense. I was still writing stories, and I had started another novel.

That year I wrote a story about a man and a woman sitting in their bedroom and watching Ray Milland in *The Lost Weekend.* It was a turning point for me, that story. All the things I had written and thrown away over the years had been leading up to the writing of that story, one that was called "Facing the Music." By then I had found some other mentors, a few other role models: William Faulkner, Flannery O'Connor, Raymond Carver, Cormac McCarthy, and Charles Bukowski. Along with Harry Crews they were the writers I admired most, and still do.

Two years later I was offered a contract for ten stories, and I sent them, and the book was accepted, and my apprenticeship period was finally over, after seven years. Harry's had been ten, and it wasn't lost on me. When my publisher asked me to suggest some writers they might send galleys to for blurbs, I named my Mississippi friends Barry Hannah, Ellen Douglas, Jack

Butler, and Willie Morris. And I asked them to send a galley to Harry Crews.

Some time passed, the galleys went out, and the blurbs began to come in. My editor sent them to me as they came, and we were glad to have them. And then one day she mailed a postcard to me, a postcard that had come to her from Harry Crews, and he had responded kindly and favorably as well. I was grateful to my friends, and grateful to him. But I never thought of trying to write to him and thank him. I figured he was a busy man, and I didn't want to bother him. I held him in such high esteem, and respected him and his work so much, that I thought it would be best to be just grateful from a distance, and not try to intrude on his life.

I kept writing and so did Harry. I kept buying his books as they came out. I published my first novel, and kept writing stories, and in 1990 Algonquin published my second collection. In was in October of that year when I read a review of *Big Bad Love* that Harry Crews had written in the *Los Angeles Times*. The review was good, and I was very happy to see it, but what surprised me was what he said about the first book, that in twenty-five years of writing it was the first time he'd picked up the phone and tried to call the author. He hadn't been able to get ahold of me, but I decided that I would write him, and thank him for the things he'd done for me, and try to tell him how much I'd admired his work through the years and how much it had meant to me in my struggles to become a writer. I got his address from my editor and wrote the letter and sent it, and then sometime later on a Saturday afternoon when I was sitting out in my room working, the phone rang, and it was him. I think we talked for about an hour and a half, and then we began to write back and forth. We talked about our lives, about dogs, about drinking, about women, about everything. Once in a while I would call him up and he would do the same. Eventually he arranged a reading at the University of Florida and offered to let me stay with him for a couple of days, and I quickly accepted.

He was leaning up against a wall when I walked off the plane in Gainesville, wearing a pair of jeans and running shoes and an Oakland Raiders sweatshirt with the sleeves hacked off. The sides of his head were shaved. He came off the wall easily when he saw me and offered his hand and we shook. He was taller than I'd imagined, a really big man. There was a tattoo of a death's head on his shoulder, and underneath it the legend:

How do you like
Your blue-eyed boy
now,
Mr. Death?

He got me into his black pickup and we started talking and didn't stop for several days. He drove me over to his house and I unloaded my suitcase and he put me into a spare bedroom he had. He'd called earlier to ask me what kind of beer and whiskey I liked, and he had laid in a supply of both for me. We sat and talked in the living room for a while, and out in the backyard where his deck overlooked a wild piece of land. His living room was sunken from the rest of the house and I met his old dog, Heidi, and then he took me out for something to eat. I gave a reading that night and don't remember what I read, but the place was packed and he introduced me. It was one of the greatest moments of my life. Later that night we sat in the living room and read to each other pieces from the books we were working on. The next day I went to his class with him, and that night he gave a party at his house in my honor. He treated me like a favorite uncle would, and told me that if there was anything I needed and didn't see it, to just ask for it. The time with him passed by too soon, but just to get to hang out with him for a while was a great gift that I've never forgotten. We've continued to stay in touch over the years, and I know that he's still working, that he hasn't finished his writing, that he probably never will. I'm glad for that.

It is important to have people to look up to at the beginning of your career. You have to find people who have found their own way of saying the things that you yourself want to say. It never comes easy, and I believe now that it may even get harder the older you get and the more you write. The apprentice approaches the pinnacle slowly, with much stumbling and cursing, constantly going down one-way streets and taking off on tangents that go nowhere. The incredible amount of things that have to be written and then thrown away is probably what daunts a lot of young writers. I don't think he ever thought of quitting. I know I certainly did, but something kept me going. To a large degree it was Harry Crews. Knowing about those hard early years made me see that it was possible to succeed at what I was trying to do, and it pulled the blinders off my eyes about what was required. In the beginning I thought I'd write a novel and mail it off to New York City and they'd mail me a check back for a million dollars, and it took a couple of years for me to find out that it doesn't work that way. A fluke does happen once in a while, but the person who starts out to write literature has already fixed himself with a hard row to hoe. By its very nature, literature is the hardest thing to write, because the standards are so high, and sometimes the rewards are low. It's probably nearly impossible to make a living solely from it, unless you get lucky. Most of the literary writers I know teach somewhere, and write their books in between classes and working on students' stories. Harry did that for a long time, and I've done some of it myself, even though I'm uneducated in the formal sense and barely got out of high school.

I heard a while back that he had finally retired, but I haven't talked to him in a while. The last time I saw him was a few years ago, when he came over to Oxford to read at the bookstore from his latest book, *The Mulching of America*. My friend Mark and I watched him get off the plane at Memphis, and were waiting on him when he got to the top of the stairs. He grabbed me in a bear hug and gave me a smile, and shook hands with Mark and told him how much he'd enjoyed his book, and then we drove him down to Oxford in Mark's old Caddy. I got a little drunk on him that night, and felt bad about it afterward, but he told me later in a letter to forget about it, that it went with the turf. I knew he meant it, and I stopped worrying about it. I was just glad to get to spend some more time with him.

Once when I was in Washington, D.C., rehearsing a stage adaptation from one of my novels, we had a bad day. Nothing went right and the lines were wrong and everybody kept missing their cues and it got so bad that the director sent everybody home early. Opening night was not far away, and I went down a snowy street to a liquor store and got a fifth of Wild Turkey and went back to my hotel room and tried to crawl inside it. Sometime later I dug Harry's number out of my briefcase and tried to call him, but his answering machine was on and all I could do was leave a message. I wanted to tell him how badly things were going, and ask him what it was that I needed to do. He didn't call back that night, but he did call the next morning, full of good humor and reassurance. He told me of rehearsing his own play in Louisville, and of how terribly things sometimes went, but how it all came together before opening night, and he let me know that the same thing would happen for us. And he was right. We fixed the lines, and the actors pulled things up out of themselves that we had never seen coming, and the play fit together like the pieces of a finely mitered box. He knew what he was talking about.

If not for having written a few books I would not know Harry Crews, or be able to count him as a friend. In a business that involves staying by yourself most of the time, and working uncertainly and sometimes fearfully toward an uncertain goal, the rewards can be few and far between and the very nature of the thing you are doing can cause a man to question the sanity of it. But other writers understand what you do and what is required of you to do it. And nothing matters but the finished book. It doesn't matter how much pain it costs you. You can't bitch and whine about it, you just have to do it. I think that's probably the most valuable lesson I've learned from Harry: Do the best work you can, whatever it takes to do it, whatever the price is that you have to pay.

Chattanooga Nights

IN THE SPRING of 1989, when I was still in my thirties, I was invited up to Chattanooga to take part in a literary conference, which was a pretty new thing for me. A lot of writers were going to be there, people I had admired from afar for a long time, people whose books I had read and treasured while I was trying to learn how to write.

I was pretty excited about going. I was also intimidated by the whole thing because I was still pretty green about the situation a young writer finds himself in if people like his books, the travel and the speaking engagements and the readings and the bookstores. There were some big names at the conference, and I had almost no name at all, having published only one collection of short stories. But it had been reviewed well, and I had an essay that I'd worked long and hard over, one that talked about the influences in my life that had turned me to writing. I also had a small piece from my first accepted novel picked out to read.

It had been almost nine years since I'd decided I wanted to write, and in all that time I'd been working steadily, week after week. I'd thrown out almost a hundred stories and five novels, and I'd come to realize finally that every writer had an apprenticeship period to go through, where there were years and years of hard work that had to be done, even if it wasn't good enough to publish. I'd come to know that the writer had to just keep on writing, and ignore the rejections, and work toward the day when the work would be good. I felt like I'd finally reached that day, and I wanted to talk a little bit about what that process had been like for me. I figured there would be some young writers in the audience, some people like me. The conference was the first well-paying gig I ever had, and the money they were giving me was a lot more than a whole month's salary at the fire department. What was even better was that I was going to get to hang around some other writers for three days. I would have gone for nothing just to have been able to do that.

There were a few people I knew at the conference: my friend Clyde Edgerton, and Arlie Herron, from the University of Tennessee, Chattanooga, who had come down to Oxford the year before and heard me read at the Faulkner Conference, and my publisher, Louis Rubin.

Mary Annie and I checked into the hotel, the big old Radisson downtown, one that was occupied by Union troops during the Civil War, and coming from our country home we were mighty impressed. The tall ceilings in the lobby were trimmed out with intricate wood carvings and there was marble on the floor, columns made from it, too. It was the nicest place either one of us had ever been in. We couldn't believe our luck, and if this was what success meant, we wanted lots more of it.

When we got to our room, there was a basket of fruit and cheese and a bottle of wine on the table, along with a note from the people hosting the conference, welcoming us. We hung up our clothes and broke out the wine and poured a glass apiece, and the phone rang. It was Clyde.

He said, "Hey. You know that cheese that's in the basket over there?"

I said, "Yeah?"

He said, "Well don't try to eat that stuff it's wrapped up in. That's wax."

I said, "Okay. Y'all doing all right down there?"

He said, "Yeah, but we've already done several country bumpkin things. Set the fire alarm off first thing."

We talked for a while and agreed to meet later to hang out. M.A. and I relaxed in the room some more, turned on the television to see how many channels it

got, marveled at all the towels we had. I think M.A.
took a long hot bath while I snacked some and drank
some wine and watched some television. Then we
got ready and went downstairs to meet everybody for
dinner.

Some of us walked a couple of blocks down the side-
walk in a loose group, and it was pretty stunning to me
to see Ernest Gaines and Louis going down the street
just talking about baseball like regular people. My eyes
got big seeing William Styron and Andrew Lytle and
Horton Foote in the flesh.

The dinner was great, the company was wonderful,
and after it was over we went back to the hotel and settled in the bar. It was there that I met a nice man named
Madison Jones. He said he lived in Auburn, Alabama,
and we sat at a long table and talked for quite a while.
He was kind to me and he had a wonderfully refined,
deeply Southern voice, and a great dignity about him. I
guess what I liked best about him was that he took the
time to talk to me and treated me as if I were an equal.
He made me feel welcome in Chattanooga, like I be-
longed there with all of them. I remember his kindness,
and his great voice. And back then I had no idea that he
was such a terrific writer. But when I picked up one of
his novels and started reading it, I knew again that I was
in good hands.

Since that time I've been able to form a larger picture

of Madison Jones the writer. I've found that he writes vividly, eloquently, and that his novels share the same virtues that all the best novels do: They possess a relentless forward drive of narrative while allowing the reader to witness the ordinary things of life with great clarity, weather and seasons and the land that lies around the characters. I love the way he describes the countryside, the small towns of the South, the way sun and rain and the different aspects of night and day affect the look of them. A spring storm or a cool fall day are rendered equally visual and accurately. I'm drawn to his streets full of shade trees, his desolate town squares where yellow lights shine in the gloom of night.

Another part of his talent lies in the ability to create internal conflict in people who know right from wrong, but are caught up in the events around them and swept forward in their momentum to the point where drastic actions can result. The passions of life. Madison is able to make his readers worry about what's going to happen next, so that his books are hard to put down, and stay in the mind until the next session of reading can come along. Mainly he gets you involved with his people and their struggles. Like all the best writers, he allows you to lose yourself so deeply in his work that the words on the paper begin to assume real life, the people breathing and moving and acting on their own, as if this story was simply found somewhere, fully formed, and not written page by page, month after month or year after year. He pulls off the great illusion the best writers of fiction strive for: He makes you forget that you're reading. This kind of writing is the best kind because it makes the reader stay up too late, causes him to put aside other things that need doing, makes him keep turning the pages long after he should have gotten up and gone to bed.

I think, as writers, this is what we strive for, this is why we often make ourselves miserable, trying for the right words and the right scenes, trying always constantly to stay ahead of ourselves, to tell a story that other people will want to read, to linger over and appreciate, to try and form images with words that are like pictures on a screen in the mind's eye, and most of all, to share a part in lives that are not our own, but that we, for a while, can live in as if they were. And if there is some joy and sorrow and understanding that can be shared in that, if the reader can feel what it's like to be in this human being's shoes, then we have succeeded, and that makes all those long days and nights facing a blank page and wondering where it all will come from worth it, no matter how long it takes. The steady progress of his prose compels you to read on until the end, to find out what will ultimately happen to these people that you have grown to care about so much.

His tragedies spring sometimes from the simplest

things, the ties between family, between lovers, between friends. His work has such a sturdy and unshakable foundation that everything is entirely logical and believable.

Madison Jones has been in this business a lot longer than I have. *A Buried Land* was first published in 1963, about the time I was twelve years old, not too long before his friend and admirer Flannery O'Connor passed away. In *The Habit of Being* she praises his work and talks about how good his novels are, and it is incredible to me now to learn these things, to learn that he would come to visit her and that they would sit and admire her ducks and geese and peacocks at the same time I was rolling on my steel skates up and down the sidewalks of Memphis.

I think about the time that writers like Eudora Welty and William Styron and Ernest Gaines and Cormac McCarthy and Ellen Douglas and Madison Jones have already spent laboring in the fields of fiction, and how these people decided long ago that writing was what they wanted to do with their lives, and in realizing this I am heartened, and encouraged, and fully satisfied that the path I have chosen for myself is the right one, and that it is a worthy life, and I am thankful to the people who have come before me for setting this example, for being who they are.

✦ ✦ ✦

WE WENT BACK to Chattanooga and the conference again in April of 1995, and this time we took
our daughter, LeAnne, thirteen by then. Madison didn't
look like he'd changed any. He still had the same short-
clipped beard and his voice was again a most pleasura-
ble thing to be able to listen to.

We usually took our relaxation in the evenings in a
hospitality room the conference people had set up for
the writers on the top floor of the same hotel we'd
stayed in before, where there was a full bar and plenty of
chairs. There was another Madison there that year,
Madison Smartt Bell. I'd met him at Goucher College
several years back, had dinner and drinks with him, and
we had begun a good friendship. Madison Bell liked to
play the blues on some of the guitars that were kept in
the room, and I sat with the two Madisons in real com-
fort for several nights, content to talk and sip a little
bourbon and just enjoy the company. There's never
much time to relax at a conference and after you talk to
folks all day, it's nice to be able to sit back and relax
with some of the people who do what you do for a living, who stay alone in rooms by themselves for large
portions of their lives and craft stories and novels.

By the time that spring rolled around, I had been to
many other hotels for many other conferences in many
other cities, and I wasn't as starstruck as I used to be. I'd

found out that other writers, no matter how famous they were, were just people like me, people who told stories for a living. In that hospitality room there were plenty of stories to hear, told by those who tell them best.

I got M.A. and LeAnne to come up one night, and we introduced LeAnne to everybody. I told her, "Honey, I know you can't appreciate this right now, but you're in a room with a lot of people whose names are going to go down in history for the books they've written."

I remember her grinning in her shy little way, and talking to people for a few minutes, and then saying goodbye to everybody. Then her mother took her back down to our room so that she could watch a movie. And then I remembered that I didn't know anything about any of them when I was thirteen, either.

I mixed another drink, eased again into my chair, and thought about how fine a thing it was to be able to sit with these people for a little while, these who are so much in rooms of their own, alone with their thoughts and the people who live on the page. I thought about how much alike we all were, whether we lived in Tennessee or Georgia, Alabama or North Carolina. What we had in common was that we loved the land and the people we came from, and that our calling was to write about it as well as we could, to find our own voices through the years of learning, and to bring forth whole people whose lives surrounded us, whose stories were told by us, and who, for whatever length of time it took to compose a piece of fiction, *were* us.

It was a good evening. I sat in my rocking chair close to Madison Jones, and felt quite at home.

Billy Ray's Farm

I T WAS FOUR O'CLOCK when I found the black heifer with the white face. She was lying down behind a brushpile below the two big sweet gum trees, and I thought it might be time. When she stood up I saw the long tail of the birth matter hanging down. She didn't want me watching her, I knew that, so I backed off and circled around through the pasture, behind another brushpile. There's a big patch of privet hedge that I need to cut again growing all around the sweet gums, but I could kind of see her through the branches. I lit a cigarette and peered around the side of the trunk and she was watching me, having pains, trying to push. It was hard to see if the feet were out or not. They might have been out an inch or two. We were worried already because it was her first one. You never know with a heifer. You might have to call the vet. She lay back down and stayed there for a while. I was torn between watching her and leaving her alone like she wanted me to. It was January 24th and there was still a little snow on the ground in the shady patches, under overhanging branches by the fence, and on the levee where it doesn't get much sun. It wasn't that cold. It was nearly fifty degrees.

She started walking slowly away and I knew she was hurting and that I was making her hurt herself more by being so close to her. She kept trying to push the calf out and I decided it would be better if I went on and started doing the work I'd come over there for in the first place, so I walked back up the hill and got the broom out of the truck and knelt where the dry grass was thick and struck my lighter to it. The embers fell and the flames climbed the tall stalks of sagegrass and soon the fire was spreading and crackling and growing in a nice even circle. I kept it under control by beating the edges lightly with the broom. I figured Billy Ray would probably be over there by five.

We'd been burning the pasture off a little at a time on the evenings when the wind was calm. We didn't want it racing all the way across the hill and maybe catching the barn on fire. You burn that grass off when the worst of winter is over, the stuff that's dead and brown, and it clears the way for the new grass that's green beneath it. Throw some ammonia nitrate on it when the weather gets warm and it'll come up lush and thick for the cows. Or the heifers, in Billy Ray's case, five of them, all first-time mamas. I raised my head once in a while and checked on her, but she'd moved off behind another brushpile down by the pond. Billy Ray pulled in at five.

He'd been looking for this calf for about two weeks. If he had classes and stayed over at the college a few nights a week, Shane and I would go check on the heifers. It was a family thing, taking care of these animals. Billy Ray stepped over the gap and wanted to know if he had a calf yet. I told him she was trying right now.

Before he went off down there to look at her, he wanted to know how long she'd been in labor. I told him it had been about an hour since I'd seen her the first time and that she'd probably be all right, to take it easy and not get upset. I knew he'd want to call the vet if it didn't pop out like an egg from a chicken pretty soon.

He stayed down there for a while and came back and said he thought the feet were out. I said, Well, I guess she's making some progress. We didn't really know how long she'd been in labor.

We stood around and talked for a while. Some afternoons I burned grass instead of cutting up downed limbs and piling brush, or chipping the mortar off the old bricks still left in the foundation of the house my cousin's husband had torn down for me. I could always find some work to do on the place at Tula, and I was over there just about every day.

He went back down and checked on her and came back up worried, said he thought he ought to call the vet. It was getting close to five-thirty and there was only about a half hour of daylight left. I told him to go ahead and call him if he thought that was best, but that he'd better get his coat and find a flashlight because it was about to get dark and cold again.

He left and I tended to my little fire. It wasn't burning very well by then, probably because the dew had started falling, so after a while I walked down to the pond to look at her. But I couldn't find her. I didn't see her up near the barn so I went back to my truck and cranked it up. The fire was just about out. Billy Ray came back with a coat, a flashlight, and a rope halter. He'd talked to Dr. Harland and the doc said for us to try and get her up in the barn and pull the calf if she stayed in labor over two hours. I pulled my truck up to the barn and we went down through the bushes to find her.

She was lying down in some tall weeds below a tangle of downed trees and briars. We got her up and could see the hooves sticking out a few inches. She strained a few times and everything back there welled out a little, the nose trying to break through a ring of thick black skin that was already stretched tight. We both thought then that we might be in some trouble. I tried to get my hand on the calf's feet but the heifer wouldn't let me touch her. We headed her up toward the barn to try to get her in the lot.

Billy Ray was worried and we kept talking about it. I was still more for the let-nature-take-its-course plan, even though those hooves looked pretty big. I knew she was suffering, having to walk with all that hanging out of her, but we took our time and got her up the hill and into the barn without too much trouble. Billy Ray had fed the heifers in there for a couple of weeks because it had been raining.

The barn leaks. It's an old barn, pretty ragged, but he's tried to fix it up. He's mowed yards since he was twelve years old, and worked as a butcher, and hauled hay, and laid sod, and worked on a hog farm. He's saved his money, and all he's ever wanted is to be a cattleman. And it's always hurt me deep that he has such bad luck.

We had just started trying to catch her and get the halter on her when a car parked on the road and Jory, a friend of ours, walked over to help us. And it was only a few more minutes until another car and a pickup parked on the road and a couple of dark figures started walking toward the barn. I told Jory I guessed the whole family was coming over.

I got in the stall with the cow and tried to catch her, couldn't half see with that lousy flashlight and she wouldn't let me catch her. The mud was so deep you had to make an effort to pull each foot out every time you took a step. I didn't know what the hell to do. I'd pulled dead calves and I'd pulled calves with seagrass rope in the wide open spaces of my father-in-law's pasture. A cow is plenty big enough to hurt you, especially when she's in pain, like this one was. Billy Ray had the idea to try and run her up in the loading chute, but it was plain that she didn't want to go in there. We tried for a while but she just kept turning and moving away from us. I climbed back out to see who had come to see about us. Billy Ray has myriad personal connections via the telephone, like a banker or a real estate agent. There was no doubt that the news of our trouble had traveled fast, fanning out over Lafayette County through the phone lines. Some would come a-running.

Mary Annie walked up with Mr. Leslie Stewart. Billy Ray buys his cow feed from him and I used to buy a lot of rabbit feed from him. All these old folks think Billy Ray is the salt of the earth. Mr. Leslie's probably raised thousands of cows in his lifetime, still does.

My wife was wading through the mud in her slippers and I shook hands with Leslie, thanked him for coming. He had a calfpuller in his pickup and Billy Ray and Jory went back with him to bring it out to the barn. I asked Mary Annie how Mr. Leslie had gotten into the picture and she said he'd just showed up at the house and said Billy Ray had called him about the heifer and he'd told him to try and get her up in the barn. Then after he hung up, he got to worrying about Billy Ray and told his wife that he was coming out here to see about him, that the boy worked so hard to try and have some cows and a farm. She said, You know how they all are about Billy Ray.

They got back over with the calfpuller and we ran her up in the loading chute and blocked her front and rear with posts. Mr. Leslie put his hand up in there to feel for the nose. She was still straining to push it out, but he said she wasn't going to be able to have it by herself, that the calf was too big.

The problem was that this little heifer had been bred to a big Beefmaster bull. She was an Angus/Hereford cross, and she was only about four and a half feet tall. It's just like a woman having a baby for the first time, but our situation was made worse by bone structure and genetics. A big baby was trying to come through a small passage. Mr. Leslie knew just by feeling of the calf that the mother was going to need some help.

Shane showed up somewhere about then and Mary Annie left, so we still had five people to work on the heifer. Mr. Leslie had some little nylon ropes in his pockets, and he made some small loops and put one around each foot of the calf, just a little above the hoof. It's always been a mystery to me as to exactly when an animal that's getting born starts breathing. If it's not breathing inside, how is it alive? This one was breathing and trying to lick his muzzle because we pulled on the nylon ropes enough to get a look at him. But it was nearly impossible to imagine his whole body somehow sliding through that incredibly tight ring of thick black skin.

It was cold, and steam was coming out of her. There wasn't a lot of blood. Shane and Jory were standing outside the stall, shining the light through the boards for us.

The calfpuller is just a winch with a small cable that's mounted on a piece of pipe fitted with a wide yoke at the end. The idea is to get the cable around the calf's feet, snug up the yoke to the cow's butt and when everything's good and tight, push down on the whole thing and pull the calf out in one smooth motion.

The heifer's deciding to lie down was the first thing that went wrong. Her back legs had somehow gotten folded up underneath her so there was really not much to push against, but when we started turning the winch the calf started coming out, big and red and slick and steaming. The amniotic sac parted and there he was, halfway in and halfway out, hung over a post we'd put behind her to keep her from backing up. And then the calfpuller jammed.

The calf was alive and breathing, his eyes open, lying in the cold mud trying to raise his head. Everything was slick with mud and shit and the stuff that had come out with him. We were trying to do two things at once, tie the ropes up past his knees and unjam the calfpuller, and we only had one flashlight.

Mr. Leslie said the calf was going to die and naturally that scared all of us. We grabbed hold of the feet and pulled on him, and she started again, trying to help us, but he was stuck tighter than a peg and probably in truth having the life squeezed out of him by the ring of skin he was trying to come through and the post his mother was lying against. There was nothing for footing but slimy mud and it was a bad feeling to pull on him as hard as we could and not be able to see him move even a quarter inch. It was like trying to pull a tree out of the ground. I had already imagined him romping on the spring grass and getting fat on all that milk.

The cable had jammed tight against the housing, and Shane went for a hammer out of the back of my pickup and Billy Ray and I pulled on the calf some more while Mr. Leslie worked on the cable. I didn't understand how the thing worked and we kept losing those precious minutes. The calf stopped moving and just lay there. He looked dead. We couldn't move him. I felt helpless, and I knew Billy Ray did, too.

After what seemed a long time but probably wasn't, we got the cable stretched back out and hooked onto him again and slid him out into the mud. We all knelt next to him and Mr. Leslie tried to revive him, pulling his head up and shaking him, but I'd seen too many shot deer like that, tongues lolling. I didn't want to accept it and I ran my fingers down his throat, thinking maybe his airway was clogged with mucus, and I thought I felt a reflex in his tongue and jaw. I pushed up and down on his ribs, trying to make him breathe, but it looked like he was already gone. He just lay there, wet and red. A big, healthy calf that should have been trying to stand.

Mr. Leslie thought that maybe if we moved him around in front of the heifer where she could lick him, he'd come back to life. Billy Ray got him up in his arms and staggered out through the lot with him, moving in the dark and getting blood on his coat, his boots sucking with each step in the mud. Shane and Jory moved the posts from in front of the heifer so that Billy Ray could get in with the calf, but when he put the calf in front of her she just stood up and started toward the pasture. She stepped on the calf and took another step or two and fell. She got up and walked and fell again.

The calf was lying in the chute that Billy Ray and Shane had knocked together so that Billy Ray could load and unload stock as he needed to do sometimes and they were shining the light down on the calf. I still couldn't accept that he wasn't going to come to life. I got down next to him and picked up his head, wiped the mucus and blood away from his mouth and blew air down his throat, thinking of the CPR classes I'd taken. But it didn't do any good. He wasn't breathing and he wasn't going to. I finally gave up and faced it. We'd lost our first calf.

I was angry about a lot of things: that my boy didn't have a decent barn to get his heifer into to help her, that we didn't have a decent light, that the lot was full of mud, that the calfpuller jammed, that we didn't have one ourselves. I was angry that the heifer had been bred to a big Beefmaster bull whose progeny was too large to slide through the width of her hipbones. More than anything I was angry about my boy trying so hard to start a farm of his own and having everything he touched turn to shit.

THE KID DIDN'T let twenty-four hours pass before he had his hands on a two-day-old Holstein bull for forty bucks. He hauled the heifer over here from our place at Tula in the trailer we gave him for his high school graduation present. It's long and red with a roof and white spoke wheels, pretty sporty. We thought it would be the most useful gift for the young cattle entrepreneur.

I went up to the catch pen and helped him get the calf fed and for me it was a learning experience. The calf's pretty neat, black and white with long knobby legs. He was lying beside a bush and I studied him while Billy Ray was getting the heifer into the loading chute. He slid some posts in front of her through the boards, then blocked her in with some more at the back of her legs. My job was to hold her tail.

There's something about holding her tail straight up that prevents her from kicking—in this case, the calf. She took a big shit all over her tail just as I was ready to grab it so there was that to deal with, but I tried to find a place that wasn't too slick. Billy Ray walked the calf up there, kind of shoving and pulling at the same time, and the calf went straight for the back teats and started butting and drinking. She didn't try to kick him and I asked Billy Ray how he happened to know about this phenomenon of tail-holding. He said it pinches a nerve in her back or something and as long as I held it up she wouldn't kick, so I kept holding it.

He took a half-gallon bottle and started stripping the milk out of the two front teats and he had about a quart in a little while. He put a big rubber nipple on it and tried giving some of it to the calf after he'd nursed for about twenty minutes, but he didn't want it. I guess he was full.

We took the calf back to his pen and turned her loose in hers, and I felt a lot better about everything after that.

BILLY RAY'S FARM does not yet exist on an earthly plane. It is a vision of his imagination so far, and

I have no idea of the form it will ultimately take in real life, but I imagine that it is a place where tall trees grow and the deep green rolling pastures are dotted with flowers. Fat sleek calves frisk on the sunny hills and draw sustenance from between the massive hind legs of their mothers, their bags laden with rich milk as they calmly chew their cuds while the calves nurse and butt. There are clear streams flowing, and the cattle drink in the shade, their elegant necks stretched to the cold water where small fish swim and bullfrogs trumpet in the evenings. There is a solitary bull who surveys his domain from a hillside, his broad face curly with hair and his gaze intelligent, omnipotent, his eyes beautiful. His body is rippled with muscle and his swinging bag of registered sperm sways in a dignified manner as he walks. This lofty monarch has the blood of the best bulls in America pumping through his veins. The calves he sires are sturdy, heavy individuals that weigh nearly a hundred pounds at birth.

In winter the cattle are warm and happy in a well-lighted barn, a vast cathedral of timbers and stalls, racked hay, a tack room, a vaccination pen, a calving pen, a dehorning pen, a catch pen built of heavy pipe.

There is a cat—several cats—to keep the barn free of rodents and a few wandering chickens to pick up the ticks and fleas. The great center hall of the barn is loud late at night with the sound of Billy Ray's boots on the concrete, for there will be no slipping and sliding here in mud while trying to deliver a calf. Electric lights will furnish the brilliance required to work on mothers in trouble.

On Billy Ray's farm there will be total harmony, wooden fence rows straight as a plumb line, clean, with no weeds, no rusted barbed wire. A few horses will be dotted over the rich grass. Maybe there will be a big catfish pond where visitors fish on Sunday afternoons.

Each cow will have an acre of grass and the grass will be regularly fertilized and mowed so that everything is neat and orderly. The mud will be kept to a minimum. Billy Ray will work hard and his farm will earn him a living, and he will be happy, and his life will be fulfilled, and he will know a great peace in his soul such as few men have ever known. God will smile down upon him and his efforts, and the farm will hum like a well-oiled machine. There will be dogs, and life will be good.

ELI IS A WONDER. He's red and white and his hair is curly and his downward dropping horns have a nice graceful curve. He's not quite two years old and he weighs about sixteen hundred pounds.

You can go out there to the fence behind our house and scratch his old head, he likes that. He hangs around a bale of hay that's about six feet thick and he gets fed extra range cubes so he'll grow and gain more weight.

You might be surprised to find out that there's such a
thing as a bull grant. I've heard of writers getting grants,
but I didn't know until Billy Ray got one that you could
get a bull grant.

The Mississippi Rural Rehabilitation Corporation, or
MRRC, furnishes weanling bulls to deserving students
through the agriculture programs in our state's schools.
These bulls come off a big ranch down in Winona, a six-
hundred-acre spread that I understand is under a pipe
fence. The fledgling young cattleman agrees to show the
bull three times at places like the Dixie National Livestock Show, where they've got all these animals that are
the giants of their species, and after that you get to keep
the bull for your herd. Eli is registered, we got the papers
on him, and at the time we got him he was worth about
two thousand dollars. At the time we got him he only
weighed about three-fifty, and he was very dangerous.
Animals that are terrified can be very dangerous.

Billy Ray went through the process, signed all the papers, made the necessary phone calls and hooked up his
new red trailer and drove down to Winona to pick him
up. When he got back home with him, Eli was not
happy. As a matter of fact he would go crazy if a person
approached within fifteen feet of the trailer. It was one
of those things that gets worse the more you look at
it. All Billy Ray's friends and cousins wanted to come
over and look at his new acquisition, and that's to be

expected, but Eli wasn't keen on a whole bunch of company. Having backed off and looked at it and figured it out, I got the big picture. Here was a young Hereford bull, bigger than a calf, but not as big as he would be some day, and he had been recently taken from the warm udder of his mother, shooed into a barn, probably with people shouting at him, and then he had been loaded into a clanging trailer and driven eighty miles to a strange environment and he was kind of like a wild animal put in a zoo. He was, in short, terrified. All those kids came over and wanted to look at him, and he would go so nuts that I had to make them all back off so that he wouldn't fall down and maybe break one of his legs before we could even get him out of the trailer. And getting him out was going to be troublesome. I know a real cowboy wouldn't think too much about manhandling a three-hundred-and-fifty-pound calf, but out here in the Horn of Plenty, we're not real cowboys. We're just guys with cowshit on our boots. We didn't know how in the hell to get him out of that trailer.

Billy Ray had built a nice little holding pen for Eli, had been working on it for a couple of weeks. But the posts were only about four feet high, and the wire was pretty flimsy. I didn't figure he'd stay in there. It was electrified, which was supposed to keep him back, but we're talking about an animal that was in a constant state of hysteria. His bawls of anguish only deepened my dread of what we had to do.

We figured we needed some reinforcements for the actual unloading, so Billy Ray got on the phone and rounded up about fifteen people and they all arrived on a warm Sunday afternoon with ropes and things. I felt a lot better. Dan Rowsey was here, and he was Billy Ray's Ag teacher all through high school. Lynn Hewlett was here, and he once loaded up a bad bull in a back-hoe bucket. There were also a lot of Billy Ray's young husky friends standing around. I had on my flip-flops and wasn't expecting to get very personally involved.

With a series of ropes they roped him inside the trailer so that they could kind of gradually ease him out of it. I think the plan was to get him into the lot and then see what happened and, if need be, tie him to a big apple tree in what had formerly been part of Mamaw's backyard. That was only as a last resort, though. The general hope was that once he saw that he was out of jail, he'd maybe start grazing peacefully.

He was already acting like he was on some very bad drugs by the time Billy Ray backed the trailer up to the gate and swung open the back door. When Eli came out of the trailer hollering and frothing he began kicking ten feet high into the air. It was immediately evident that they were going to have to tie him to the apple tree, so they did. That worked until he started walking around and around in circles and finally came to the end of his rope, where he kept plunging until his knees went out from under him. Suddenly we were having an unscheduled hanging. I said, Well, damn, he's dead. His tongue came out of his mouth and his eyes rolled up on his head while they worked feverishly to untie the rope, and I figured he had about maybe five seconds left before death got him when they untied it and he dropped to the ground. Did I say that by then there were about thirty people watching this? Maybe it was only twenty-five.

He hit the ground and just stayed there. I couldn't believe it. A new bull, newly dead. He pretty much just lay there, not even gasping for breath. I was just standing there shaking my head. Nobody said anything much. But then he drew one breath. Then another one. In a few minutes he was able to raise his head. Somebody who was thinking fast put a halter on him, a thick thing made of soft nylon rope that was hooked into a lead with a big brass snap swivel. We just watched him after that. When he got to his feet, shaken though he was, he started going crazy again, bucking and jumping, bawling, kicking. We just backed off because he was shaking the apple tree. But I'll be damned if he didn't decide to settle down.

In short order I went and made a big jug of ice water, we all had some of it and congratulated ourselves, and everybody left except me, Mary Annie, Billy Ray, my nephew Jeremy, Michael Paul, and Snuffy Smith. And that was about the time that Eli decided to go crazy again. And it was almost worse than before. But we said, Well, hell, that big thick rope's on him, and the apple tree will hold him, but then we happened to notice that in all his exertions he had spread that brass snap swivel and it was only hanging on him. All he had to do was turn the right way and he was loose.

The good rope had left with either Lynn or Dan, a real cowboy rope that was stiff and braided, and all we had around the place was some of this plastic string that Sears uses to maybe wrap around refrigerators. You put some of that stuff around your hand and make a couple of loops around it and hitch the other end to some serious cowpower, you're liable to get your hand peeled to the bone. But it was all we had, and the boys crept up to him like commandos. They managed to get it around his neck, but the brass snap swivel finally parted, and suddenly they were taking a ride with Eli—Michael Paul being dragged, Billy Ray holding him around the neck, Snuffy with his hand inside his mouth, and then the bull fell on all of them. He was kicking and biting, and the boys were getting mashed. Mary Annie told me to *do* something. I had on my flip-flops. I jumped the fence when I saw them go down under him, leaped in— the Leaping Daddy come to correct a wrong—and grabbed a hind foot and got struck in the chest and knocked back about six feet in the air. I jumped back in there and found a place to hold to that wasn't so easy to get kicked from, and we got him up and held him in a headlock and *walked* him by main strength back to the tree and retied him. Then we fell out on the ground for a while, counting and licking our wounds. Billy Ray's ribs were bruised, my chest was bruised, and Snuffy had three fingers that were bitten and bleeding. It was the first time I became aware of the fact that a bull *will* bite you.

It took a few days of feeding him and petting him, talking quietly, but Eli finally calmed down and accepted things and we were able to take him off the rope and let him graze.

After enough time had passed, Billy Ray was able to train him to the halter, walk him, pet him like a dog. That was about a year and a half ago. I go out there now and scratch his old head. I hope he's forgotten those bad early days when we were just getting to know each other. Because he could sure put a hurt on you now if he decided to.

I DON'T RECKON bad luck ever takes a vacation. It doesn't for Billy Ray. I had to go down to Tampa for a few days and I got back on a Saturday night. A friend of mine was passing through town and he stayed

Sunday night with us, and then I got back to work on my novel.

I got ten pages written and at four o'clock I got in the truck and drove over to Tula to check on the heifers. The black one was missing and I didn't know if it was time for her to have her calf or not. I thought she might be up in the barn, or down in the bushes, so I started walking over the place to look for her. She wasn't in the barn, wasn't down by the pond in any of the brushpiles of downed timber. It was cold, and it had snowed some the night before, and I had my good Tony Lamas on tramping around in it. I found one damaged place in the fence, but it wasn't big enough for her to squeeze out of, and I couldn't figure out where she could be. There was a little lot next to ours and the owner had let Billy Ray's heifers graze on over into it, but I took a look over there and didn't see her.

It started snowing and it was pretty beautiful. Big wide flakes were drifting down onto the surface of the pond and they didn't even make a ripple. The snow started sticking and I kept walking around, looking for that heifer. I was worried that I wouldn't find her, and I decided that she had to be lying down in some spot that I'd overlooked, but it was getting dark, and colder, and I stopped on the levee to watch the snow drift down for a while. There was total silence, and the cedars were green, and my boat was pulled up on the bank, and the dock had snow dusted all over it. I went on home and told Mary Annie that one heifer was missing, but that I'd go look for her first thing the next morning.

THE SUN WAS SHINING the next morning, but it was bitterly cold. Shane had told me the night before that there was no fence on the back side of that lot next to ours, and that the heifers could wander off down in the woods if they wanted to. I'd said to myself, Well, damn, my luck, that's where she is.

I drove over to my little place at Tula and headed down through the bushes he'd told me about and immediately saw a big black form lying on the ground. The heifers had made trails down there like deer. At first I thought she was dead, then I saw her move. When I got up a little closer I could see the calf sticking out. My heart sank deep. She was lying against a cedar tree on her side, quivering or maybe having convulsions. The calf was black and his head was resting on top of his feet and his swollen tongue was protruding from his mouth. It was easy to see that he was dead, but impossible to know how long. I started running and I ran back to my truck and drove fast back home to get on the phone and call Mary Annie and get her to call the vet and ask him what to do. I was afraid I'd have to pull the calf myself and I wanted to save as much time as possible while I started gathering up what I would need: some rope, a long chain, my three-ton come-along.

She called back and said the vet was in surgery and would be for another hour and a half. He said the calf would have to come out if we wanted to save the cow, so I knew what I had to do: hitch the come-along to a tree with the log chain, put some ropes around the calf's feet, and try to get it out without pulling it in half. There was nobody to help me, but as bad as it was going to be, it had to be done.

I had to kind of gird my loins on the way back over there. Sometimes you can't understand why everything has to go wrong. Maybe if I'd found her the day before. Maybe if it hadn't been snowing or maybe if I hadn't written all day and could have gotten over there earlier. Maybe if the boys had told me there were a couple more acres of woods the heifers could wander off into when they got ready to get in trouble. Or to go even further back, maybe if Billy Ray never had bought the damn things in the first place. You can run all that stuff through your head over and over, but it doesn't accomplish anything.

I drove as close to her as I could, then started carrying the stuff through the fence. Going down through the bushes with it I had to bend over and collide with branches. I had to keep my gloves on to keep my hands from stiffening up.

The come-along is a heavy, cumbersome tool, made out of cast iron and a steel cable and a couple of high-strength metal hooks. The idea is to hook one end of it to something that won't move, like a building or a tree, and hook the cable to what you have to move and then work the ratchet handle, which is made of thin conduit pipe that will bend if you overload the three-ton capacity. That's six thousand pounds. You can get your truck unstuck with it, or pull a tree out of a pond, as I've done several times. I knew it would pull the calf out but I didn't know what it might do to the cow. But if I did nothing she would lie there and die.

It might have been a little easier if I'd had my chainsaw to clear some of the brush, but I had neglected to bring it. She was facing with her head to the left and I tied the log chain around a little tree and stretched the cable out. I had a big four-foot nylon fish stringer that was about a quarter inch thick. I tied it onto the calf's feet, above the hooves, making two overhand knots at the ends so that I could put the hook of the cable into the middle of it. Part of the amniotic sac was dried to the calf's head. I pulled that away. He'd been dead long enough that the hide beneath it was dry and fluffy. I ought to go ahead and say now that I talked to myself and the cow for the next hour and forty-five minutes, and anybody who could have walked up behind me and heard that might have thought Larry needed an emergency trip to the funny farm.

When the cable first tightened, the calf moved a little, maybe an inch. Some steam started coming out of the heifer and then all my cable was gone, and I had to unhook it and make a smaller loop around the tree with the chain. I took off my gloves and ran my fingers up inside her to see how much space there was between the birthing walls and the calf's body. I couldn't get my fingers in up past my wedding ring. There was nothing to do but keep pulling on the ratchet, keep taking up the slack, over and over.

The heifer was groaning and moaning. Once in a while she'd lift her head and roll her eyes. I couldn't rightly imagine the amount of pain she was going through, so I tried not to think about it. A similar feeling used to come over me when I was with the fire department and working to get somebody out of a crushed automobile. Just do the job as fast as you can. But that ground was cold, just like the air, and there was a good chance she'd been right there ever since sometime Monday, and if she'd been real unlucky, maybe Sunday night. Had she had a drink of water in all that time? Hell no.

The calf came on out maybe three or four more inches, and then I was out of cable again and right up next to the tree I'd hooked to. So I had to find another one, move everything again. I knew that the natural movement of a calf being born is out and down, since the cow is usually standing. The angle I had was straight out. So I moved to another tree about four or five feet above that one to try to pull the calf at something more like a forty-five-degree angle. I didn't know if that would work any better because I figured that most of the fluid that's supplied to ease the birth had either already dried on the outside or was backed up inside, behind the calf. All the lubrication was gone and after I tied the chain again and started moving the ratchet handle, the calf didn't move but the heifer did. She started sliding across the ground toward me, pulled by the force of three tons. I felt like just sitting down and crying. I knew I was going to kill her. Billy Ray was off with Eli at the Dixie National at Jackson and didn't even know any of this was happening. All he was going to come home to was some more bad news. It didn't seem right for anybody to have such terrible luck.

There was nothing I could do but keep working, but after a solid hour of pulling that handle and moving the chain to different trees, all I accomplished was to get the cow turned a hundred and eighty degrees and the calf halfway out. And it looked like he wasn't going to come out any farther. I couldn't tie the heifer's head to a tree because that would kill her. Or pull the calf apart.

I didn't know what else to do. I thought about going back to the house and calling the vet again, get him out here, maybe go get one of my older friends who knew something about this, but in another way I didn't want anybody to see this, and I didn't want to give up and admit that I couldn't do what needed to be done. So I sat down and smoked a cigarette and rested. I looked everything over. The heifer was lying within two feet of a big cedar tree with her rear end pointing toward it, the same tree she'd had her head almost up against when I started working. I said, Hell, if you could get her up against that tree with the calf in the open, maybe the tree would stop her from moving and the calf would come on out once you put the force on it again. Any vet reading this will probably see a lot of things I did wrong, but I was just trying to figure it out. All she was doing by then was lying there and shivering, so I moved everything around again and found a little cedar back up on the bushes and laid it all out straight, hooked to it, and slid her up against the tree. When her hind end came to rest against it, she stopped moving, and the calf stretched out tight. I talked to her. I told her, This is it, baby, I'm either going to kill you or get that dead thing out of you, and I may do both. I was scared to pull so hard. I didn't know how much pressure that little dead body could stand. But everything got very tight, and it was hard to move the ratchet. I worked it slowly, one notch at a time. Then it all jumped loose and I saw that my big fish stringer had snapped in two.

I never have a whole lot of sense in a situation like this, generally run around in a panic, but this was a rare occasion and I had realized before I left the house that the fish stringer might break, and I had gone into the utility room and untied a big yellow braided nylon rope that stays tied to my wire mesh fish bucket. I tie it to my boat when I'm fishing to keep what I catch alive until I'm ready to dress them. The yellow rope was in the back of my pickup and I ran back across the pasture to get it. I made the same loops, tied them to the calf's feet, and hooked it all up again. The heifer let out a bawl when I tightened it up and I worked the handle a few more times. It couldn't have felt good to her, but it must have been some kind of relief when the calf slid out all black and smoking, the hindquarters wet and shiny, the beautiful little feet streaked with white and looking soft as cheese. The placenta rolled out immediately, followed by a couple of quarts of bloody fluid. We both just rested then.

After a while I got up and pulled the calf away from her. It was a little heifer, and if anything it was bigger than the red bull we'd lost a few weeks before in the barn. That chilly wind was still blowing and although the sun was shining down on that little glade, the dead calf gave me a feeling of gloom so deep I didn't have much hope for her mother. I didn't figure she'd be able to get up, and without a helicopter there was no way to get her up out of those woods.

It was getting close to three o'clock by then and it would be dark in a few more hours. I dragged the calf over to the fence, under the wire and up to my pickup. I let down the tailgate and got up in the bed of the truck to lift it inside. It wasn't as hard to load up as a grown deer. All my stuff was still down in the woods with the heifer and I had to make a couple more trips to get everything out.

The lives of cows are fickle and uncertain. One day they may look fine and the next day be dead as a hammer. They can stumble in a creek and never get up or out. They'll find a bag of fertilizer stuck back in some place you thought they couldn't reach and eat that, fall over dead. Get out in the road and get hit by a car. This particular accident is doubly unfortunate for the owner of the loose cow, because not only are you out the money the cow was worth, but also liable to have to pay for fixing somebody's vehicle. Hitting a cow at about forty miles per hour will mess a car up real good. So I was already having a pretty bad case of what I call the Dead Cow Blues. She probably wasn't going to get up. It was going down to freezing that night and she was going to have to lie there shivering and shaking, suffering, all night long. And she might have to stay that way for three or four days. Unless. Unless I went home, loaded up the .357, and put a bullet into her brain.

But it wasn't my cow. It was Billy Ray's cow, and he didn't even know what was going on.

The first thing to do was dispose of the calf. I drove down on the Cutoff Road, stopped in the bottom next to the bridge over Potlockney Creek, and dragged the calf out of the pickup and into the tall weeds beside the road. I knew the buzzards would clean the calf up in a few days. I took my rope off its feet because even though the calf was dead, the urge to go fishing would always come again.

I was pretty morose driving home. Even if the vet came out, what could he do for her at this point? Could he give her a shot or would he advise me to dispose of her humanely? I was willing to do that if I absolutely had to, and I would have to if he said so, but I wasn't going to shoot one of Billy Ray's heifers just on my own judgment. Neither did I want her to just lie there and suffer and suffer and suffer.

LeAnne, my twelve-year-old, had come in from school by the time I got home and I'd had no food in me all day long. There was a little smidgen of homemade brown whiskey that a friend of mine had sent over on a UPS truck from Alabama, and I got a shot glass of that and checked the messages on the answering machine. Billy Ray had called home the night before and learned

of the missing heifer, and he was having another one of
his fits, trying to place a collect call on an answering
machine three times. Oh shit. I got them old Dead Cow
Blues. I damn sure wasn't going to call him up at the
Holiday Inn in Jackson while he was getting Eli ready
for the show and lay all that on him. I was going to tell
him, just not right then.

I told LeAnne she had two choices: She could leave
the answering machine on and ignore Billy Ray when
he called back again, or she could take the collect call
and lie to him and tell him she hadn't seen me, or had
seen me but didn't know what was going on. I'd already
told her everything that was going on, what the heifer
and I had gone through, the blood and the guts in the
woods, et cetera. She was watching one of her sitcoms
on satellite and fixing herself a sandwich and made an
easy decision—said she'd just lie. I wish I could make
decisions that way, in a snap, and not have to agonize
over everything the way I do. I took the whiskey back to
my room and called up Mary Annie. I often have to rely
on her for cow advice since she grew up on a farm and I
didn't, and she has driven tractors and chopped cotton
and had spent most of her young life, the part that happened before I came into the picture, chasing and doc-
toring and feeding cows.

We talked for a while and the conversation wasn't too
cheery. The vet had doubts about the heifer ever getting

up, just as I did. So, inevitably, the subject of maybe having to shoot it came up. I told her I hated to have to do it and she said she'd do it. We talked about Billy Ray and what he was going to say. I told her about the fit he was having on the answering machine. I thought it was pretty ironic that he could smell a rat all the way from Jackson. She told me to go back and check on the heifer and she'd talk to him, try to calm him down. I hung up and sat in my chair for a minute, looking out the window. There was no doubt in my mind that the heifer was a goner. It was probably going to degenerate into a situation where the only question was whether to let her die slowly on the frozen ground or put her out of her misery.

None of that made me feel any better. I got the revolver out of the bedside drawer and put some bullets in my pocket and went back over there in the pickup. She was still down and shaking all over when I reached her. I figured she was dying. I thought about walking back to the pickup to get out the gun and shoot her. I thought maybe it wouldn't be too bad if I leaned in close and averted my eyes. But what if it didn't kill her? I know some guys who shot a cow in the head with a .410 slug one time and the cow tore down half the barn and ran off in the woods.

What to do? What to do? Let her lie there and suffer, or stop the suffering? Call the vet? It was almost dark.

I doubted he had any miracle drug that would make her jump to her feet. I wound up giving her a drink of water and going back home. I gave myself another drink of whiskey.

MARY ANNIE LAID the bad news on Billy Ray that night.

I had to get on the phone with him for a while and listen to all of it. He wanted to know why his luck was always so bad and I didn't have an answer for him. He was a hundred and fifty miles away and he was supposed to show Eli the next day and he said he was coming home. I told him he couldn't, that he had to show the bull because it was the third time and after that, Eli was ours. Don't you come home, I told him.

I'm coming, he said. No you ain't, I said. Don't you come home.

It took a while but we finally got him calmed down a little. We told him we'd see him the next night and if the cow was still alive by then, there was still some hope left. I told him I'd go check on her the first thing in the morning. We hung up, and I could only shake my head over how truly bad his luck was. Two deliveries, two dead calves. Billy Ray's farm wasn't working yet.

THE NEXT DAY I was up early. I grabbed a cup of coffee and hit the door, drove over to Tula and sprang down to the woods. I was fully expecting to see her stretched out dead, but when I got down close to her I could see that not only was she alive, but she had managed to move about three feet away from the tree. I ran and got a bucket of water from the pond, lying on the icy boards on the boat dock and dipping it full. I knelt next to the heifer and trickled the water into her mouth. Her tongue was long and gray and I could hear it going down her throat. The swelling in her side had gone down some and she actually tried to get up on her knees. I definitely wasn't ready to shoot her then, and I even felt a little better about everything. But she was still down. I got down next to her and tried to roll her over onto her belly, thought she might be able to get up if I did that, but she was too heavy for me to move. I thought of cranes, tractors, slings. It was a jungle down there. By that point I was ashamed to call the vet since I'd let her lie there all night already. I knew that Billy Ray was coming in that night and I decided it was his baby, I'd let him decide what to do. But she did look better than she had the day before. I came home and worked for a while, then went back and checked on her again, gave her some more water. It crossed my mind to give her some hay, but I didn't. I didn't figure she'd be able to eat, stretched out on her side like that.

We tend to have these long, involved family discussions in the kitchen where everybody gets to put their two cents in. That night when Billy Ray came home, it was pretty bad. His mother had told him to sell the three other heifers, had already told him to sell the other four after the first calf died, but sometimes he's like me, stubborn as hell, and trying to talk to him is like trying to talk to a post. But he called up Rodney White and got him to agree to come over the next morning and pick up the other heifers and haul them to the sale in Senatobia and try to get part of his money back before they one-by-one slowly keeled over and died in childbirth. He mentioned his cow trouble to Rodney, who had been in the cow business a very long time, and Rodney told him to get six ounces of turpentine and a pint of mineral oil and mix it together and pour it down the heifer's throat and it would thin her blood and she'd probably get up the next day. Suddenly the air was electric. Hope had sprung anew!

I'd put a big ham in the oven just before I had departed for my last cow-checking of the day and it was on the table along with black-eyed peas and macaroni and french fries. The boys and LeAnne went ahead and started eating so they could go over to Tula and load up the heifers, haul them over here and turn them into the lot where they'd be ready to walk into Rodney's trailer the next morning. The kid had already loaded his bull and pulled a trailer all the way from Jackson, unloaded him, and now he was hauling cows after dark.

His mother and I just forgot supper for the moment and got into the T-Bird and hit the road to town, in search of turpentine and mineral oil.

We had to go to Super D, of course, wandering up and down the aisles among the toothpaste and hemorrhoid ointment for something I was pretty sure they didn't even sell. But we found it, in tiny blue bottles, the turpentine plainly marked HARMFUL OR FATAL IF SWALLOWED. Hell, this shit'll probably kill her for sure, I told Mary Annie. But on the other hand, I thought, maybe it's not harmful or fatal to cows. We grabbed the mineral oil and got out of there and drove home fast. I found an empty Wild Turkey bottle under the counter and mixed it all up in the sink. The boys took it to Tula and poured it down her throat by the weak glow of the same flashlight we had used on the little red bull we lost.

I was apprehensive and uneasy in my bed that night, hoping our luck would change for the better. I dreamed of cows standing on their hind legs going in and out of the pasture in a rusted red trailer, with their horns and hooves poking out, waving like people you see pictures of on those topless two-decker buses in England.

NEXT MORNING SHE was still alive. The water had frozen in the bucket and I tried to smash the ice with a stick, but finally had to beat it against a tree to break it and give her a drink. I walked over to the barn and gathered an armload of hay and offered it to her, and she became agitated and began drawing the hay into her mouth with her long gray tongue, grinding it on her back teeth, and I knew then that I should have done it sooner. Some of the stems were more like sticks and I pulled them out of her mouth and kept kneeling next to her, giving her a drink of water once in a while. I kept watching her eyes. I couldn't read any pain in them, and there was no way she could express what she had been through. If I stopped feeding her, she would reach for the hay that was on the ground, pulling it in with her tongue. I sat beside her for a half hour, feeding her, then I gave her a final drink of water and piled all the hay up next to her where she could reach it, and left.

I'm sitting in my room now, the dogs sleeping on the bed behind me, Sammy Lee and Lilly and Hallie, and snowbirds are feeding from the little birdfeeder that I loaded up with seed a few weeks ago. I wouldn't let my dogs suffer the way I let that heifer suffer. What does that say about me? Does it say that I care about some animals more than others? Maybe it says that I know that some are kept as only potential makers of supermarket meat while others sleep in my bed and are like my children to me. Does it say that I'm a bad man, an uncaring man, or only uncaring in certain ways? When I let Sammy sit in my lap while I'm typing these words on this machine does the thought of shooting him ever enter my head? He snuggles under the covers with me at night. The cow does not. He doesn't worry about anybody ever eating an offspring. And neither does the cow.

But I hope she's still alive, and maybe even a little better. I'd like the Dead Cow Blues to leave for a while, take a nice long vacation.

IT DIDN'T WORK. She didn't get any better. The next day when I went over she couldn't even lift her head, and she was too weak to drink the water I tried to give her. The heifers all went to Senatobia in the big red trailer of my dream where they brought a lot less than Billy Ray paid for them. He lost $250 on one heifer alone.

Sometimes you just have to do something. I opened the drawer under the microwave in the kitchen and showed him the Smith & Wesson, strapped in its little brown leather holster. I told him the bullets were on my dresser, and he went over there to do what had to be done.

IT SNOWED YESTERDAY and we drove by the place last night on our way to town. We had to go to a party and life has to go on in the midst of whatever else is happening.

Billy Ray and Allan, a friend of his, had cut the fence and dragged the dead heifer onto our place, and somebody from the county had come out to bury it with a backhoe. The snow was all over the ground and the backhoe was sitting in the middle of the pasture with the lights on and it looked spooky, everything white around it, and the lights shining on the bucket, the big claw stretched out on the hydraulic arm like some kind of prehistoric beast that was gnawing at the frozen ground.

BILLY RAY DOESN'T tend to sit around and mope over a setback. The next morning he was up early and out cutting pulpwood with Allan, trying to recoup some of his losses. Mary Annie met him driving the log truck and she said he waved to her and grinned, sitting up high in the truck as if he were saying, Look at me, Mama, I'm doing something I like. I'm happy.

Counting the dead heifer and the two calves and the reduced price the heifers brought at the sale barn Thursday, the kid lost about fifteen hundred dollars, or about half of all the money he had in the world.

ELI, THE HEIFER and the calf she adopted, and one other cow, are over here at our house but there's no stock on the place at Tula now. Not much point in burning off the rest of the grass since there won't be anything there this spring to eat it. I won't go back much until it warms up and I can get out with the chainsaw and start cutting the scattered limbs from the ice storm, or chip some more mortar off the weathered bricks that are left in the toppled chimney that's lying in big chunks on the ground.

I'm scared for him to buy any more cows just now. I couldn't stand to see him get burned again this quick. He just got another job cutting meat at a supermarket uptown, and he'll probably keep cutting wood for a while. School won't be over until May. He'll do all that and keep saving his money, although it costs him a good bit to feed Eli. I don't know how big that bull will get but he's still growing. He can eat one of those big six-foot-round bales of hay in about a month. Once the grass comes out he'll be able to graze, but this cold weather seems locked in for a while longer. A few of the birds have already returned, some cardinals, a few sparrows, and the other day I thought I saw a little female bluebird sitting on the feeder. They just don't stay around here in the winter. The birdbath is frozen, nothing but a big rim of ice sitting in the scalloped top. I can see a big hawk cruising over the dead brown grass from here. He's probably having a hard time of it, too. But spring will come. It won't always be cold and frozen and there won't be a skim of ice over the pond at Tula. The stubs of last year's okra stalks are jutting from the ground in the garden where Lilly has gnawed them down, along with my grapevines, and my blackberry bushes. She's a boxer and letting her inside is like turning a horse loose in the house.

I hate it that Lilly and my other dogs have torn up the whole backyard, dug up flower beds, just gnawed everything down in general and torn some of the screens off the house. But I wouldn't swap any of that for my dogs. I can always plant more vines and bushes and things. I can fill the holes they've dug with a little dirt. It's a small price to pay for the pleasure they give me, the warmth of their personalities and their endless amusements. They never make nasty comments the way some people do and they don't have to be excused from the room if they need to fart. They don't ask for much, just for you to like them and feed them and give them a warm place to sleep on cold nights. In many ways their company is much more preferable than that of a lot of people I run into. But I can talk to them and they can answer with the expressions on their faces, their wagging tails, their obvious happiness at being with me. They're so easily satisfied, and their needs are so simple. You can smile at them and they'll smile back. You can't have a relationship like that with a cow.

THE FICKLE FINGER of cow fate swings wildly and it's like a roulette wheel, you never can tell where it will stop. You are sometimes not even aware that it might be hovering near you until it lands, with full force. I mean you can be minding your own business with no idea that anything untoward is coming toward you, and then, boom, there it is.

Events were going on outside my peripheral vision: Billy Ray had one real cow left, a big Brahman with long drooping ears and a kind of mottled hide, brown fading to gray, and big wet eyes that when you looked at them inside a cattle trailer seemed immeasurably compassionate and sad. She was off up in the pasture behind the house one night in the beginning throes of calfbirth, and I was in the house messing around with some of my stuff, looking over my manuscripts, listening to some music, not really working but really at peace with the world since it seemed that most of our cow problems were over. The loss had been taken and the future didn't actually look bright but it looked like we might be able to back up and regroup for a while, plan the next strategy. Maybe buy some grown cows. Maybe not even worry about cows for a while. There had been so much grief that it was best to put it away from me for a while, not hold it close to my heart.

So this cow started having a baby. I didn't know anything about it. Billy Ray went up there to check on her and found an ominous large wet sac of something membranous and semitranslucent hanging out of her. He started having another fit and he came back down here and told his mother that he thought the uterus was hanging out. Prolapsed. The uterus gets messed up and if you've ever read any of those James Herriot books you know what I'm talking about and what the cow has to go through to get it put back in and what the vet has to go through to get it put back in and I didn't know anything about all of this going on.

Some phone calls were made. They were keeping me in the dark, protecting me. They often do that. Sometimes they don't inform me that things are approaching the crucial stage. Often they wait until the crucial stage itself actually arrives, and this was the case here. Billy Ray and his mother called Dan Rowsey, described what was hanging out of the cow, and Dan was forced to give a diagnosis over the phone. Since Billy Ray had described the thing hanging out of her as *gray*, Dan said he thought her uterus had prolapsed with the calf behind it. He told them there was only one thing to do: load up the cow (it was a Sunday night), haul her up to the vet's office, let him perform surgery on her, then get rid of her. Mary Annie came back here into my nice warm unmolested nest and laid that on me.

I didn't say anything. I felt a little bitter, true, but I've learned to develop a kind of fatalism that takes me through a lot of storms. One of the things I do is tell myself, when things are looking pretty bleak, no matter

what hour of the day or night it is, that tomorrow will
be a better day, even when I know that tomorrow won't.
I also console myself with knowing that my children
need my help and that's my job. So I pulled my boots
on. Grabbed my coat. Didn't bitch. Got my cap and
my gloves and my flashlight and went out to get in Billy
Ray's truck for that bad ride up into the pasture. I
couldn't imagine what the thing looked like. I had
something in mind kind of like half of an unborn ele-
phant, maybe, hanging out, the big grayish mass swaying a few feet above the ground and the cow carrying
on in some kind of horrible way. Bawling, swinging her
long gray-brown ears around. The nightmarish logis-
tics of the rest of the night were too bad to even think
about. And the vet bill. How much would that be?
What if the vet was watching a world premier movie
on TV? With his socks on? With a glass of wine in his
hand? Would he want to drop all that and go into the
smelly guts of our cow? It just gave me a bad feeling all
over but I got into the truck without protest, everybody kind of walking on eggshells around me, waiting
for me to blow up. They knew that being disturbed in
my happiest of happiests by real bad news was one of
my least favorite things to happen on a Sunday night.
You've done your work then. Even God said that was
the day of rest. You shouldn't have to go chasing after

bawling cow guts on a Sunday night. But I didn't say a word.

We got up there and put the light on her. A small clear bag of fluid that held about a quart of water was hanging out of her and I breathed a big long deep sigh of relief.

"Shit fire, Billy Ray," I said. "She's fixing to have this calf and she just ain't busted her water yet."

I went back to my stuff, pulled my boots off, put my feet back up, turned Leonard Cohen on.

NEXT MORNING I moved over close to the window with the field glasses and focused on the cow out in the pasture, a small brown-gray lump lying on the ground behind her. Billy Ray had tried to get up close to the calf to determine its sex but the cow threatened to kill him, so he backed off. I could see pretty good from here. The calf had a white face and it turned out that she was Eli's first calf. The calf got up on its knees and I saw the long red umbilical cord hanging down. Hawks were cruising the sagegrass and my dogs were playing in the yard. I had a cup of coffee and I was listening to Bruce Delaney. I kept the glasses to my eyes like a field marshall or a killer of long-distance game. The calf wobbled around some but that was to be expected. It was walking pretty good to be only about ten hours old. It put my mind to rest and all I had to worry about was making one day follow the next. I knew I could do it. I lowered the glasses, let them hang around my neck by the strap, and looking out over the pasture I lit a cigarette. Life seemed to have regained its balance. There were no cows suffering anywhere because of me.

Fishing with Charlie

H E WAS STRAIGHT FOR thirteen months, hadn't even had a beer in all that time. He'd lost the needle and he was singing good and feeling good and blowing the sax good, and the day he pulled up in the yard and parked, one of the first things he did was show me a beautiful old Remington .22 pump that his daddy had given him a long time ago. I had some beer in my truck and he had some Cokes, and we got in and drove over to a twenty-seven-acre impoundment that a friend of my daddy's had built back in the 1970s sometime, a place that wasn't fished much, a place that was loaded with largemouth bass.

It was and is a wonderful, almost magical lake. High bluffs wooded with oaks and hickories rise up over the east side, and the water is dark yet somehow invested with a strange clarity that often lets you see the fish when it strikes. A couple of boats stay tied to the levee, and we availed ourselves of one and slipped out into the

smooth ripples with the sun bright overhead, not a hot
day at all, just a great day to fish. Charlie was a worm
fisherman, a diehard. He had some kind of half-floating
white-speckled things he called grubs, but they were
more like fat Texas worms, only weirder. We paddled
around and he got into the fish immediately. He talked
a lot but he didn't talk loud. What tickled me was how
he'd set the hook. He'd lean way back when a fish hit,
and you'd think he was going to fall out of the boat, but
then the fish would be hooked and Charlie's arm would
be cranking on the reel and he'd tow it in. I was fishing
with a small floating Rapala, getting a strike once in a
while, but mostly I was watching Charlie because he
was knocking them dead.

We fished all that evening, talking and catching up
on each other's lives, paddling around on the dark water, and wherever he threw, they hit. I guess he caught
about thirty, but he only kept eight small bass for fillet-
ing later that night. We hooked up with Tom Rankin a
little later at my pond and got into my aluminum boat
and drifted around for a while, didn't catch anything. I'd
stocked it but they were still small. Full of bream but
no grown bass yet. A big thunderstorm came up out of
nowhere, complete with jagged streaks of lightning, and
Charlie allowed as how we'd better get our asses out of
the water, so we did. Tom snapped a picture of Charlie
and me on the dock I'd built with my own hands.

I had a foil-wrapped package of ribs from Handy Andy and we took them over to Sheila Baby's and microwaved them, and broke out some potato chips and paper plates, and sat out on her deck looking at her big lake and eating the ribs. She had a chandelier made of mule deer horns hanging over her dining-room table that I thought was about the coolest thing I'd ever seen.

Her driveway was muddy and we almost didn't get out of there. We had to pick up a bunch of heavy rocks and weigh down the back end of Tom's Dodge to make it out, slinging mud everywhere, laughing together the way only good friends can.

I REMEMBER CHARLIE standing on the stage alongside Duff, his whole head and hair slicked back with sweat, blowing on that saxophone and the whole house rocking. And then he'd start singing in this old black man's voice, low down and dirty, and he could wail. He loved my books and I loved his music. The Tangents were the house band of Mississippi, and Duff had these cowboy boots that were patched with silver duct tape. They were the best I ever heard.

I can segue into a perfect place with my guitar when I've had enough to drink and it's quiet at night and my work is done for the day and I know that all I have to do is stay up late enough to be able to sleep. I don't worry about the sun rising over the window because it doesn't matter, because I don't work for anybody but myself. But in those small quiet moments of early morning, I miss Charlie. And I'm not pissed off at him for doing what he did, only greatly saddened that he left us so early. He was thirty-nine.

ENTRY FROM MY journal, April 14, 1997: Got up at 12, read some on the novel, marked a few pages, started mowing the back yard at 2:30. Stopped at 4:15 to go to the feed mill for soybean pellets. Ate some ribs and mowed again till almost dark, unloaded 600 lbs. of feed and watered the heifers, burned two woodpiles behind Mamaw's shed. Started to work, ate supper, worked until nearly 11. Tom called late and said they'd found Charlie Jacobs dead in New Orleans. What a waste.

The journal entry doesn't tell about me crying in the kitchen, but I did.

HE'D CALL UP and at first you wouldn't know who he was because he wouldn't tell you. He'd just keep talking and asking you how things were and after a while you'd realize who that gravelly voice belonged to, and even if it had been six months since you'd seen him, he'd be talking just as if the last conversation you'd had with him had been last night. He'd always want to know when we were going fishing again.

Who can say what his life became in New Orleans?
The band had broken up after so long, after all those
years of playing frat parties and smoky bars and wed-
dings in the Delta and private gigs for friends. Fish went
to work for Larry Stewart, playing the keyboards, and
Duff had to stop drinking, and Charlie drifted down to
the Crescent City to play solo gigs and form a new band.
He had been writing some songs and he wanted to cut a
record. I heard from him rarely; he was busy with his
music and I was busy with my writing. Tom would talk
to him once in a while and give me a report. It was ru-
mored that he was back on the heroin, but I didn't know
if that was true. The one thing he wanted from Tom was
a copy of *Father and Son* to read, and I know he asked
for it several times. I was in New Orleans last fall and
should have looked him up, but I didn't, should have left
a signed copy for him at Beaucoup Books, but didn't,
just caught another airplane and went on with the book
tour. But I know he got his hands on a copy somewhere and read it, and I heard what he told Duff about
it: "It's a damn good book." Unquote. Hell, that's a good
enough book report for me.

 ‧ THE LAST TIME I saw him was in a bar in Oxford and we talked for a while, standing there at the end
of the room. He had a new woman with him and he
looked wild and fragile. But he said that things were

going well in New Orleans and that he had good hopes for cutting his record. There were always a lot of people wanting to talk to Charlie and we eventually drifted away from each other that night. I never talked to him again.

HE LIES NOW in his family's burial ground, an Indian mound that stands looking over a big field where cotton is probably growing right now. On the day of the funeral it wasn't planted yet, but we've had a cold spring in Mississippi, and everybody's late planting.

I rode down from Oxford with Jonny Miles and Tom, and we were drinking beer from roadside gas stations before eleven o'clock. We knew it was going to be a long day, and we fortified ourselves frequently. We made it to the church on time, and the little yard was filled with musicians and writers, artists and photographers, the family and friends, and anybody else who loved the Tangents and their music, and Charlie.

From the church we drove in a long procession of cars through Delta fields where tractors were moving over the flat land that stretched for miles and miles. We all ended up strung out on a long dirt road that curved away into the distance and where willows grew beside the road, and most of it was flat except for that mound where the tent had been set up and people had already started to gather. It took a long time for everybody to get out of their cars and walk up that dirt road, but they waited until everybody was assembled and then the preacher said his last words. After that, and after the flowers had been taken from the lapels of the pallbearers and placed on the casket, Duff and some of his friends gathered in a small group at one end of the tent and stood on the plastic grass and they played. They played soft and sweet and low, and everybody knew it was their last gig with Charlie. There were no amplifiers or electric cords, just the gentle sounds of acoustic guitar and banjo, drifting out over the warm April afternoon, where the tractors still rolled through the fields. They played four numbers and then they stopped. And then we all began to go back to our cars, to break apart into our little groups.

Sometime later that night we found ourselves at Duff's house, where a bunch of players and pickers were sitting on milk crates or kitchen chairs, and that was as far as I made it into the house for quite a while. The paintings that Duff had started doing were hanging on the walls all around them, and they were drinking beer still, as were we, and I just sat there for a few hours and listened. I knew that I was witnessing something profound and beautiful, and that the music these men were playing was the means for them to deal with their grief. So I listened reverently, quietly, and just before it broke up I went into the house for a while to speak to Duff.

He was subdued and somber, giving one of his kids his spelling lesson. We talked some, and then it was time for us to go.

The night sky was full of stars and wind was moving slowly through the trees outside Duff's house. The players were packing their instruments away and lingering in the driveway for last words, last handshakes, and we stood around with them for a bit, just making small talk, trying to express to them how much difference their music had made for all of us on this special day. The players were out of beer and I had a few half-cool ones still left in a sack in Tom's floorboard, and I handed them out and they thanked me for them. We got into the Toyota and rode back through the black Delta night, past the little towns and the lumbering trucks, the cotton fields and all the land that was spread out before us on both sides.

A few days later Tom gave me a big print of the picture that he had taken of Charlie and me on my boat dock that day. It's in black and white, very clear focus, and he's standing above me saying something and I have my face turned up, listening to him. I don't remember what it was that he was saying. I wish I could. But I've got the picture up beside my desk, and I remember the music, and the hot Mississippi nights when he stood pouring sweat on the stage and let it rip, playing his heart out because the people were screaming for it and because he loved it so much. I'm grateful for having known him, and happy that he thought enough of my work to call me his friend, or to go fishing with me. I'm glad we had the quiet times as well as the loud ones, and I hope he's finally at peace out on that Indian mound, overlooking his beloved Delta, the land of his blues.

So Much Fish, So Close to Home
AN IMPROV

I T STARTED OUT simply enough as nothing bigger than an enjoyable evening of listening pleasure: Oxford's Kudzu Kings jamming at Proud Larrys', six-buck cover although the doorboys kindly don't charge me. It's a bennie, might look tiny to some people, but over a year's time it adds up. Like cow feed.

Things out at the farm were relatively cool but not as cool as they might have been. My bad bull was in my neighbor's pasture, running herd over his herd, having laid some serious whipass on his bull and run him off into a remote and unpopulated corner of his own kingdom, where he probably had to stand under a tree and watch the great-horned Omar mount in rapid succession the mottled members of his former harem. You get a bull firing in seven seconds but with a stud horse you might have to stand around and watch it for twenty minutes. If you can stand to. Don't get reincarnated as a mare.

RIFF: I'd just spent three hours of the
previous Saturday morning, just as the
Rebels were getting ready to play the
Memphis Tigers at Vaught-Hemingway,
chasing on foot and tractor my neighbor's
peek-a-boo cow back into her own pasture
through the same thirty-foot section of
rotten and downed posts and rusty wire
from which Omar had made his escape.
Bobby Ray had helped me fix that hole or
I'd helped Bobby Ray fix that hole and I just
hadn't figured out yet how to get him back
on Mamaw's place, being he is large to the
tune of a little over a ton with the
aforementioned wicked sweep of armature
and a way of throwing his old head up high
when you approach that makes you think
twice about getting up close to him
without something between you and him
to climb up on or get behind like a tree or a
fence or a barn. It's the kind of thing that
worries your sleep, your animal which you
after all are responsible for, being on
somebody else's place, because you might
be subject to damage charges or maybe have
to listen to some legalese if something
happened like say he went through another

fence and got on somebody else's place and
either tore up a turnip patch good or gored
some hapless goob.

It was fairly dark inside Larrys' as usual and fairly
crowded as well. My perch away from the undergrad
gabfest taking place on the floor was one step down from
the top of the steps at the back where people kept not
seeing me and bumping me with their legs. I was just
glad to be there. I'm a big Kings fan. Some college girl, a
redhead in black twirlies, didn't see me and kept her little behind right in front of my nose for three or four minutes, but nobody thumped any cigarette ashes on my
head. Cervantes was at his usual post in the corner with
his cane, behind the hole in the bar where the beerboys
carry in their suds, and he got me a Coke with lots of ice,
nice heavy glass, made me feel like a millionaire.

Soon enough the Kings took the stage to shouts
of approval and claps but I couldn't see very well
from where I was. About that time Mustapha-who's-
moved-to-Chicago-now came up and said why didn't
we move down to the empty pizza kitchen and then
K-Martwanda came up and said the same thing, so,
wham, we moved.

In there it was a pretty good advantage point. It was
true that you couldn't order drinks from in there because you would've had to scream your head off and

that doesn't work with a bartender and they don't appreciate it I know, but there were empty tables to sit on and we were right across from the band guys who were having about as much fun gigwise as any band guys I'd seen in a while while ripping out some legwettin' riffs. They played one song about how we still don't have cold beer in the stores in Oxford, which always reminds me of the story about Faulkner getting all broke down like a big she-elephant at all the old tightassed graybeards who used to run Oxford and voted beer out during World War II and telling them, I'm sure with much disgust and righteous indignation, "Only reason you son of a bitches got to vote beer out is because every able-bodied man who could have voted to keep it in is over in Europe fighting your war for you," or words to that effect. He might have said more, I don't know, he might have mentioned pity and honor and sacrifice and compassion and all the old verities and truths, but more likely he was just pissed that he was too old to fight himself and couldn't get a cold beer in a café anymore.

And sure, I'd gotten up about high noon that day, I don't deny it. That was usual, too. Like Robert Earl Keen I like to sleep late and stay up late, like he tells an audience on one of his records. No telling what Robert does when he stays up late. Aw, he probably writes songs and plays his Martin. I like to do that, too, and read and drink coffee, smoke a few Marlboros, eat some ice cream, maybe catch a documentary about something like Benobo chimps over in the Philippines or wherever they live who, when they get nervous or frightened, have sex with their mothers or aunts or cousins or sisters only for some strange reason not known to man they never have babies from that, like something in their reproductive organs has a primitive brain and knows this doesn't count, is that too far a stretch? no? well, more and more people kept coming in but of course it didn't affect us in our protected section. You could see over that wall pretty good if you stood on your tiptoes. But even if you didn't you could see Bukowski's and Tolstoy's heads and Groover's and Dos Passos's heads. You could hear Guitar Bojangles back there playing his lap steel even if you couldn't see him. It was way cool and we listened to every song they played. They played a bunch of them and then some other they turned the lights on and suddenly, like always, it was past time to say, Hey brother can you shag me another cup of mead?

Then the barboys are clearing it out:

"Let's go, people."

"Bar's clooosed, everybody, let's gooo."

The things you see at closing time. Some pretty Ole Miss coed's flopped over a table and she's puked on the floor some puddinglike stuff a strange color like psychedelic purple and if you're not watching then you step in it, only then realize what it is and see her, harsh lights shining on her, her nice diamond bracelet, her purse hooked onto her arm, it's hanging down, where're her friends? People kicking beer bottles along the floor amid the cigarette butts. If you walk by the front door at three A.M. it's open and all the stools are upside down on top of the bar and silent black men are mopping and sweeping while the streets are deserted and the cops are all parked somewhere now that there's nobody left to nab.

Somehow there was still some billiard action going on down the street at Murff's. Mustapha went to the bar and I sat down at a tall table and started talking to Lorna and she started telling me about the big fish deal that was going to be happening down at the spillway on Enid Reservoir in the morning. She said it only happened once every five years. She said they were going to shut the spillway down, close that concrete hole tight, and pump the water out of it to check for cracks, and that there were going to be hundreds, possibly thousands of fish suddenly stranded, and that the General Public would be down there waiting behind a fence, and that at nine o'clock they were going to let everybody in the bottom of the spillway to grab all the fish they could for free. I went Wow, man. I got pretty excited and started envisioning things.

Paddy Chayovsky came by and shook hands. Rimbaud from Ajax came by and shook hands. But it got

time to be out of there, too. I talked to a few of my ex-
students and some of us walked outside and stood
around waiting for everybody to come out since we
were all going over to Grover's house to see what happened. Grover is a superstar.

I wanted to know lots more about the fish deal and
Lorna filled me in with plenty of details in my car
driving the long way around to Grover's house with
Paddy in the back. I had a cut of "Sin City" with
Dwight and k.d. and we drove by Mr. Billy Faulkner's
spread. Nothing down there had changed. They hadn't
totally screwed up Oxford. Not yet. But pretty soon
they would. People were coming out of the woodwork
from all over America to move here because of all the
culture in town. They were being encouraged to. They
were being lured. And the streets were getting filled
with more cars and more people and condos were going
up all over everywhere, even in places you wouldn't
think a condo could go. I was born here. I remember how
it was when I was a kid. Maybe that's just waxing nos-
talgia. Things are better in some ways and worse in others. There are just too many people trying to live in this
little place, hence your high-dollar town houses and the
awful gnashing of treehuggers' teeth. There is probably
nothing that anybody can do about what is coming.

Lorna said the last time they'd done it, shut the spillway down like that, that it was kind of like a gold rush,

and that there'd been fishblood and fistfights in the midst of a fishgrabbing frenzy. I could imagine stinking heaps of bream and carp, maybe bulletheaded behemoths in torn T-shirts standing in them, bloodied, with fishbillies in their hands, the weeps and near-orgasmical moans of a grandmaw in a cotton housedress, a big buffalo lodged and wiggling dumbly between her thighs, others wading forward to help, clubs raised. I could smell the blood and death of it, could see how the sun would be shining down on the carnage at nine o'clock in the morning. Would the soaring September temperatures rise and would tempers rise within them and incite them to fall upon each other, excited by the orgy of death? Would they be clubbing each other's toes in the bloody water? Lorna said you could get little ones for your pond. I said I wanted big ones for my skillet. She said reckon I wanted to go? I said, Aw shit my damn bull's out, I got to go home and see about him.

> **RIFF:** During the course of the evening I'd been recalling the gist of a conversation relayed to me by my spouse, Marlana Antonia, one she'd had with our neighbor just that day. She knew about me spending that hot morning running nimbly through Mamaw's pasture without benefit of water or coffee, trying to chase the cow out, and

later, in the neighbor's pasture, trying to
chase the bull back in. We ran over hill and
dale. They scooted easily from shade pocket
to shade pocket, waiting for me to catch up
with them, but like the mouse with the cat
batting him around I soon grew tired of the
game. My neighbor had come over and told
Marlana Antonia that he had the bull up,
that all his cows had come down close to
his loading pen and that he got them all in
there some way, maybe tolled them in with
a bucket of feed or something, and that he'd
managed to let the cows out and keep the
bull in, so I was already thinking that if I
stayed up late that night and went to sleep
and didn't get up until late the next day, my
bull might have to stand in that pen in the
sun without maybe any water until I got
my dead ass up and went up there to check
on him. If he hadn't broken out of the catch
pen I was going to take him to the sale at
Pontotoc and sell him. I was going to sell
the few other bovines I had, too, because I'd
paid a lot of money for them, and because
they weren't making any money for me,
and because I needed money, and because
I'd gotten pretty sick of having to feed them

on cold muddy bitter rainy days in
February. So I knew I couldn't go to sleep.
But we were going over to Grover's, and I
knew they'd all probably stay up all night.
It didn't look like a problem. The only
problem I could see was the possibility of
maybe Omar hurting me in some way,
stepping on my head or crushing me up
against a fence or a tree or poking a horn
into some of my internal organs. It happens
to bullfighters all the time, rodeo clowns, et
cetera. Some people have actually gotten a
horn up their butt, you could look it up but
I don't know where.

Grover's "pad" or "crib" is down on a small street
kind of on the northern portion of town, a quiet neigh-
borhood except for whatever racket Grover makes
on his stereo. I don't think he has police problems yet.
His kitchen is about as big as a kitchen table but three
or four people can glom in there and manage to get ice
from the freezer and freshen drinks and let folks in and
out of the bathroom. You see books in Grover's house
and he's got a piano in there that he plays in savage
bursts of intensity. The night I was there he had
recently broken his guitar and I noticed that by picking
up a splintered part of it that still had two tuning

pegs attached, and you could still read "Silverto" at the top.

I think Grover likes this place because it's kind of secluded and easy to miss and it's fairly dark down there. There are lots of places like that still in Oxford, a place where one can be hard to find at night.

We went in and people started drinking and Paddy Chayovsky sat down on the bed and started playing a guitar. There were seats to sit on and Grover showed me an old American banjo that his parents had bought him in Zanzibar or somewhere, and we figured out finally that it had probably come from some sailor on a ship in World War II. Grover screamed for his bottle and somebody passed it to him. I was nondrinking at the time, working on getting some of the wrinkles out of my face, and I did not begrudge the great joy it gave my friends, whoa no, was only glad to be among their cheerful fellowship and their shouts of laughter.

Salinger and Melville and Frederico and Hester came in and we all kept talking. Some of us moved to the front porch for a while and I spent some time sitting on a beer cooler with Lucinda, who was bummed out because Grover wasn't talking to her very much. We discussed her dog and her newsletter. We moved around and took turns on the couch and at some point somebody went for some more beer. It got pretty loud and rocking, what with Grover's stereo and the instruments in the house, including the piano, which Grover would sometimes beat on, resulting in a kind of primal music, but only when he got frustrated, and I wondered about him breaking the guitar. I decided that he had to be either crazy or very talented, so I decided to loan him my little Fender Squier Bullet, black and white, in the case with a strap and some picks, knew he wouldn't hurt mine but needed a simple axe to play.

Paddy Chayovsky didn't exactly have a sinking spell but Paddy Chayovsky got kind of sleepy later on in the night and curled up on Grover's bed right there beside the front door and pulled a white bedspread over himself and went to sleep. The party went on and on. The party was sucking a lot of things in but it wasn't spewing many things out. Cigarettes were being consumed, the packs getting thinner, and the beer was dwindling and the consumption of it proportionally so. I saw Melville asleep on the porch and saw Lorna slip a pillow under his head. Salinger had sprawled on the couch, the sheer size of his body staking undeniable claim to it, for all night, if need be. Once in a while he moaned.

Lorna and I sat on the porch for a while and talked. In the kitchen Mustapha discussed the merits of Slobberbone. I told Grover that I had a guitar I wasn't using and that I'd drop it by sometime. He was glad to hear that and assured me that he wouldn't beat it up against the wall like he'd done the old Silvertone from which I'd found the remnant. He talked some about how difficult it had been to smash it into so many small pieces. It had something to do with Grover playing a piece so perfect on the guitar that he feared he wouldn't ever be able to recreate it, and the course he took was the only one he saw open. Apparently it had been a pretty methodical guitar-smashing. Apparently there'd been some stomping involved as well. I didn't ask him if there were any more pieces of it left, or if I might have one of them in case there were.

But alas the crowd dwindled. Some people have to work in the mornings. Others march to the beat of their own drum and are akin to little lost waifs that scatter down the street like the gingko leaves every fall at the corner of Madison and North 14th, hurried by a colder wind or a harkening toward daybreak. When our friend Frederico's legs failed him he was taken quickly to a waiting pickup truck, whisked crazy-legged away across the dewy grass, and banished from sight by a dying rumble of pipes in the dark as the pickup pulled him to another place. I stood with Grover and Lorna in the street, eyeing the advent of dawn. It was only something purple over the bypass. But coffee thoughts were getting 3-D: a hot white paper cup, bright lights inside a convenience store, while outside the yawning workers were gassing up and hurrying, dawdling not much, facing another day for more dollars. Salinger stirred on the couch when we said his name but I thought he might have another nap or two left in him.

The big fish grab looked out of my grasp. I hadn't been up twenty-four hours yet, but by the time I got done with the bull shit it would be getting pretty close. Would it be possible to go home, get him home, then go down to Enid Spillway, forty-five minutes from our place? It might be. It might not be. What if free fish were in abundance and I missed it and what if, later on, Lorna and Paddy Chayovsky showed me pictures of coolers full of catfish on ice, their whiskered mouths, their dead eyes? Would I wail and grind my teeth then? Oh yeah.

Lorna mentioned smokes and I mentioned my coffee thoughts and soon we were making an early run. Salinger raised up from the couch and asked if he might get a ride and we invited him to hop in. Grover was a lean figure in the yellow square of light in the doorframe, calling out for cigarettes. Lorna squeezed into the back and Salinger lowered himself into the bucket of our white Pony for the ride home.

The streets were almost deserted. Only a few cars were beginning to stir. The early morning street workers, you see them. They're out in their trucks or pushing a handcart around the square to make a city pretty in the rising light.

Salinger said he'd had a long night and was going to

bed. We wished him well and hail fine fellow well met at his step and Lorna got into the bucket he'd vacated.

We went to a place that used to be a small grocery store, but now it's a green-and-white BP just like any other BP in the whole similar country. If you were blind-folded and driven there over the course of a few days you might take it off and stand in the parking lot and won-der if maybe you were somewhere off the interstate in Pennsylvania, since they have pine trees, too.

We got our stuff. Lorna paid for my coffee. I wouldn't let her pay for my cigarettes. It didn't seem like a thing to let a lady do. And just as we were getting back in the car I got a call on the car phone, an instrument with which I'm not real familiar. Lorna kind of helped me figure out how to answer the thing, and when I did, it was my daughter, Louisa Latigo, wanting to know where I was and when I was bringing the car home. I told her where, asked her how soon she'd need it. It turned out that she needed it in twenty-five minutes so she could get to school, so that was a mandatory book, right out of there into growing traffic.

On the way back I told Lorna I didn't know if I'd make it down for the fishgrab or not, that my main pri-ority was getting my bull back on Mamaw's place. There was no telling how long it might take or how much success I might have or even if he was still in the catch pen. Unless it was real strong he was probably already out of it. If he was in it I'd have to get the heavy cattle trailer hooked up to my very lightweight ancient Asian pickup, a faithful little one that poots a bit of smoke, a machine that never once failed to do anything I asked of it except go forward a few times when there was some mud under the tires. It might be hard-pressed to pull a hefty bull's big behind.

I let Lorna out and told her that maybe I'd see her. She walked away toward the house and I drove into the morning, scooting around the edge of town and going right out into the country, driving faster than usual but still under the speed limit. I was home on time and Bobby Ray was getting ready for work. I was pretty much a sleepyhead but couldn't hit the bed. I sat on the front porch in the swing. I drank my coffee. I played my Martin. I waited for the sun.

THE MASSEY-FERGUSON is red, has big black tires and horses numbering fifty-three. It's a bad little mother at fourteen five, cheaper than a lot of pickups. It weighs in at fifty-eight hundred pounds and driving it down the road in fourth gear at twenty mph is like riding a motorcycle without a helmet. It's not a real stable vehicle and a man needs to be careful driving it. The sun was up and starting to shine bright when I took a towel out to the tractor and wiped the dew off the seat. Omar was right across the fence in the northeast corner of Mamaw's pasture, behind a line of cedar trees whose low

limbs extend out almost twenty feet from the old fence
that Marlana Antonia's daddy built so long ago. Wood
rots, wire rusts, trees fall in high winds or ice storms.
Out here in Y'Cona there are cows all around and some
of us have cows close to each other and everybody has a
bull or two and sometimes the bulls get too close to each
other and begin a bellowdance and then they can fight
their way right through a fence. It can get pretty brutal.
They can become bloodied. You wouldn't see these cowboys trying to ride them if they weren't tough. Or maybe
just one cow will find a broken spot in the fence that sep-
arates two landowners and cross over. Omar escaped
from our place at Tula the first day we got him and ran
loose in the woods with a spotted heifer of mine for almost two weeks before Mr. Leslie got them into his barn
and Marlana Antonia helped me hook up Bobby Ray's
cattle trailer and go down there and get them.

> **RIFF:** Marlana Antonia had an amusing
> conversation that day with a man named
> James who was down there helping. James
> was evidently somewhat nervous around
> the cattle and Mr. Leslie had all kinds,
> bulls, cows, calves, steers, heifers, you
> name it.
> **MARLANA ANTONIA:** Which one of these cows are
> you scared of, James?
> **JAMES:** I'm sked a all of em.

I had on my rubber LaCrosse boots with the fancy camo tops and drawstrings for the wet grass I'd soon be tramping through. The tractor took me up past our own rotten catch pen and down the pasture road and over a hill where an old house once stood that used to hold rabbits and their nests within its walls and across the dry creek carefully because of a treacherous slope, scary to climb when muddy, across the other pasture and up past the pond where pond perch worked their wonky fins and under the cedar trees there he was, just on the other side of the fence, huge, horned, damn near walleyed, the bulk of him black but wearing a white blaze face and four white stockings, kind of almost like some kind of fancy racehorse except that he's bovine instead of equine, and he was bawling for our cows still in Mamaw's pasture, his jilted lovers lowing back at him still steady and indomitable, bereft of his concubines but probably not a depleted potentate, done bred everything of my neighbor's that was ready to breed, looking as he always had like he might explode at any minute, old Grasshopper, Red Rock, Huey's Lewis News.

Sun up and not murderous on the head because of a bad head like so many other mornings but each blade of sagegrass shining with moisture in a field of wet misted grass. I'd seen Lorna rub her goose-pimpled elbows as morning had crept toward completion. Had they gone for the big fish grab, I wondered, or had the lure of the pillow cried too loudly? Surely there was no other fool but me who'd been out all night without sleep and was now messing with a bad bull. I got down off the tractor and approached him. I kept the fence between us.

Cows are incredibly dumb things. They'll crap on their food while they're eating it, will stand on it and eat it and crap on it and eat it some more, yet they make such lovely cheeseburgers. And woe goes to the lowly part-time cattleman who thinks he'll throw fourteen cows and a bull into a pasture and soon start cashing fat checks from the sale of milk-fed junior beeves. They die having their babies and the babies die, too. They fall into holes and don't ever get up. They get out in the road and get hit by cars. They have to be caught and held and in-oculated, dipped, dusted, palpated, deflated, dehorned, castrated, artificially inseminated, weighed, wormed, fitted with tags, or chased down by the vet when they throw out their uteruses. They don't have enough sense to get in out of the rain. They're a large disappointment to a man who wishes a carefree existence in this world.

I approached him slowly, speaking calm words of en-couragement. There was a wire gap somewhere along the fence, and if I could just get it opened and somehow get behind him without spooking him it might be pos-sible to herd him gently back toward where he be-longed, without getting too close to him. I be a man who be scared of his own bull.

But it wasn't to be. I crossed the fence downwind and made a big circle up past some abandoned farm machinery and crossed another fence that was only two strands high and then I was in the actual pasture with him, no fence between us, him eyeing me carefully through the screening elm branches and scattered privet hedge trees. He was still bawling lustily to the cows and they were still answering him, but it didn't sound how you might think it did. Ever since I've owned this bull I've noticed that his bawl is more of a strangled-sounding goat-yodeling than anything else.

I tried to move cleverly and he moved the other way and got off a little ways from me so that I felt safe enough to walk up to the fence and open the short gap and let it drop to the ground. He had his out now and it didn't look like there'd be any need for any fencecutting or -mending if he would just look over there where I'd just been and see that open hole and walk through it. But a bovine is so stupid he can't even look at something like that and figure it out. He went the other way, his dewlap swinging, his horns bobbing, a homesick bawl rising in his throat.

> **RIFF:** Year before last he lost the tip of his
> tail. Bobby Ray told me either a cow was
> standing on it when he stood up or it
> dropped off from fescue poisoning. I found it

out in the pasture one day and kept it in a
drawer in my desk for a while, a dried
hollow tube of skin with long silky
yellowed hair. I'd take it out and show it to
people and they'd marvel over it, but it
wasn't really good for anything. I think I
finally threw it away.

I circled wide and turned him and waved my arms
and he went back up the deep ditch he was in and got
to within fifty feet of the open gap and stopped and
wouldn't go anymore and looked back at me like, Okay
dude, what up? I stopped where I was too. I knew that if
he decided to run over me there wouldn't be too much
I could do about it because after chasing him over the
pasture that Saturday morning I knew he could outrun
me and I didn't know if I was still agile enough to get
quick like a monkey up a tree. Impasse. The cows were
still bawling. Then I got a bright idea. Why not leave the
gap down, circle back the way I'd come, get on the other
side of the fence where my tractor was still sitting and
start hollering "Sooksooksooksooksooksooksook!" like
I do when I'm feeding them in the winter, get all the
cows stirred up some more, get them to bawling louder
and get him even more stirred up and entice him even
closer to the gap and just let him walk home?
It didn't work exactly that way. I got around there

and hollered all that Sook thing and the cows got to bawling louder and running toward me and they crossed the creek and he got more and more agitated and got up close to the fence and started pushing against it and I heard the posts start cracking and then suddenly like the light-footed gazelle he jumped the whole thing flat-footed and never even hung any of his belly hair or his penis sheath and then they were all reunited happily back on Mamaw's place. I closed the gap, got back on the tractor and started it, then headed for the house, wondering how many coolers I had for fish, how much ice I would need for a king's ransom of tabby cats.

YOU CAN KEEP all your crawfish pie and your shrimp and grits. You can give me some of your Blue Point oysters on the half shell and about half your turtle soup, but mainly give me fish, bream or crappie or catfish, even bass, fried, with some taters on the side, a small brown mound of hushpuppies, but mainly—and some ketchup—give me crisp meal-coated flakes of fish, white and steaming under the tines of the fork as it twists the once-swimming flesh from the thin bones. Don't even hand me any of that coleslaw because I won't eat it. I'd be needing some lemon wedges. Louisa Latigo is like me in that.

Then imagine if you will a vast deep hole in a concrete ground, with barely slanting walls, and a big flat parking lot up on top where a gigantic crane sits at rest, and helmeted construction workers and state park employees who scurry or cluster or simply lean on a fence looking down to what is happening below.

It was hot as hell, about ten o'clock, and the lines of cars and trucks stretched so far back from the spillway that I'd had to park a good ways distant and walk up to where all the action was evolving. I carried in my hands a fish basket, and my rubber boots were still on my feet. But my toes were sweating in the heat, and them boots weren't made for such walking. I should have been home in the bed.

It had been an unbelievably long night and it seemed even then a bit hallucinatory, to have gone through so much and still be up for more adventure. I walked by trucks and cars and trucks and cars and even some vans, which made sense: more hauling space if they were getting them out by the bathtubloads.

What was bugging me out was that I was an hour late. Even on the grass trucks and cars were parked, and they were parked on both sides of the road that led up to the spillway, but all the vehicles were empty, no folks inside them at all. The crane didn't appear to be in action. What was it for? Who the hell put it there? Were they going to haul fish up with it? I wanted to demand.

A large bunch of people were all hung in a row on a makeshift fence that bordered the spillway, and I spotted two T-shirted figures among them, matching shirts, white and red letters. I recognized the golden locks of Lorna, and the dark fuzzy head of Paddy Chayovsky. They hadn't failed to show up but they didn't seem to be completing their mission. It was way too hot for somebody who hadn't been to bed in a long time to be staggering around in it. But once I got up beside them, I could see what they saw. And it took my breath away.

Out yonder beyonder lay an open rock chasm with a wide flat bottom, and shallow pools of water lay in it here and there, and it was sluggishly moving with people and fish.

They were scooping them up in plastic laundry baskets.

They were shoving them nose first into cardboard barrels.

Some had those big serious garbage cans on wheels.

Children were shrieking with laughter and their high cries rose on the wind and drifted up to where we stood. I reached out and touched Paddy Chayovsky on the shoulder.

"Hey, you made it!" he said, and I cut to the chase on my bull story while he nodded grimly and listened. Lorna gave me a hug and smiled gamely, but the toll of a night without sleep was beginning to tell on her face. Paddy Chayovsky, with his impish grin, appeared to be pretty fresh. I was beginning to move pretty slowly, but I thought I could probably bolster up some quick energy if it meant filling the big coolers in the back of my pickup.

We didn't talk much. We just watched the people scooping up the fish. I could see a line of sandbags like stairs going down beside the wall of the spillway into the bottom below, and people where hauling up great barrels and containers of fish: buffalo, bream, catfish, bass, carp. There seemed to be generous amounts of fishslime on everything. And something even more exciting: Down near the mouth of the spillway there was a deeper concrete pit, and the water had been drained down to a depth of about three feet. Men and boys with nets were down in it wading, and large fish they had thrown out lay gasping for water on the concrete lip above them. That looked like the place for me. I asked Lorna how long the people had been in there and she said about an hour. She said they were waiting to get some small fish to put in a pond, and then they led me around and introduced me to a guy who worked there, sort of a park ranger guy, I guess, with a helmet and a uniform and patches. He told me pretty quick that if I wanted some fish I'd better get down there in them pretty quick. Below us the people were still moving through the pools of water where the fish splashed and tried to escape, but of course there was no escape. Some construction dude with a helmet on his head walked by me carrying a catfish that had to weigh fifteen pounds.

The heat had gathered into a big white ball above us and it was burning me down. I saw a lady park ranger in a uniform and she had a helmet on, too. It all looked real official.

Lorna gave me her dip net and she gave me a small Styrofoam cooler with a lid that looked like a new one. I told them I was going down and they wished me luck.

So off I went into that teeming mass of humanity, through a gap in the fence that had to be the one Lorna had mentioned the night before, the one that kept the crowd back until it was time to go in for the fish. It was that woven stuff that you put up to keep in sheep or goats or calves but it's not too good for bulls.

> **RIFF:** Not that Omar got out of wire like
> that, only that it's not much good for bulls.
> The year before, he went through some of
> that stuff going after one of my heifers, and
> nailed her, too, but suffered an I-kid-you-not
> serious laceration of the actual calfmaker
> itself that had me worried for quite a while,
> until I saw that it looked like the flies
> weren't going to blow it and cause it to get
> infected and maybe rot off.

It stretched way out there, in a big semi-circle, all the way across the banks of the spillway and across the bottom of it way on down there, and then back around the side so that it encompassed completely the spillway proper. I guessed they'd been pretty serious about people not getting in there early, and in my mind I compared it to a yard sale, where lowlifes are knocking on your bedroom window at four A.M. and the bastards are asking if they can have a certain lamp they've checked out by flashlight for two dollars instead of three.

I headed down that sandbag staircase, and I began to see that there'd been some real work going on around there for quite a while, getting ready for this day. Halfway down I paid some attention to an enormous blue pump that looked like it might have come out of the belly of a ship. It was set up on a platform on timbers, resting on a big bed of sandbags. There were cables going up to the crane, and I could tell they'd been using the pump because water kept leaking out of it. And a whole bunch of workers were down in there, too, more guys with helmets, and some of them were grabbing fish. People were coming up past me constantly with pails and garbage cans and washtubs and cotton sacks and steel barrels and plastic barrels and wet cardboard boxes and watering tanks for livestock and even wheelbarrows full of fish, all dead, all looking a little brutalized, a lot of them covered with slime and blood. And down below, the big fish grab was still in full flailing fury. Overweight teenagers with their pedal pushers rolled up past their knees and old women with those funky knee stockings like the ones Marlana Antonia has started wearing in the last few years were wading in the little pools where fish slapped the thin water and tried to leap, mauling and grubbing and grabbing. Old geezers wobbled goggle-eyed, stunned by the smell of blood or maybe just approaching sunstroke.

Once down in the bottom, I found the wet rocks slick and treacherous, and fish already captured lay stacked in piles everywhere. I saw some tiny catfish too small to grab, a waste of time, their fins so ribbed with razor-sharp bone that they'd get tangled up in your dip net and then you'd be playing risky business trying to get him loose with an excellent chance of getting your *Yow!* impaled and the worst part is having to pull it out of your living flesh with it sucking at that thing. So I skipped those pools and edged closer to the pit, where the men were still wading. I looked up to see Lorna and Paddy Chayovsky high above the concrete walls, looking a little like movie stars with their matching Ray-Bans. They waved at me and I waved back with the dip net. It was beginning to look like a lot of the fish had already been grabbed, and maybe even most of them.

I walked around the pools some more, but most of

the fish in them seemed to be shad, trash, not fit for anything but bait. I hopped from rock to rock and the pickings started to look pretty meager. Lots of small fish flopped around. All the big ones up there had already been captured, that was easy to see. The water wasn't over a few inches deep anywhere. That had to mean that the rest of the big boys were down on that deeper end, where the real fishdaddies were still wading. I walked over that way.

You could see them grabbing for food, and their ejaculations to each other or to friends or family members on the fence above were amplified within that concrete cavern and those voices echoed back and forth inside the walls, and made things appear even more frenetic, more frantic. A man with a longhandled net slashed out at a truly giant carp, golden, bobbing, escaping. Two others shouted and grappled together with a live thing beneath the surface, but it knocked them loose and evaded them. There was a problem getting down in there: There was a slick and steeply slanted wall that looked to be the only way in. What they were wading through was over my boots easily, but, if I took them off, who knew what broken bottles there might be on the bottom? Stuff in wallet, watch? Dead and dying alligator gar lay taking the full heat of the morning sun all around me, their bony snouts alive with the rapacious flies swarming over them, buzzing their evil songs.

I saw that you'd have to get on your butt to slide off down in there, and you wouldn't stop until you got to the bottom and how were you supposed to get out? Were they going to bring in ropes to haul people out? I stood there, wracked by indecision, and then suddenly my decision was made for me. The lady park ranger, who had come down the sandbag staircase to stand beside the pump, had a bullhorn in her hand, and through it she said, pretty forcefully: "All right! Everybody out of the pool!" She meant the pool we were in. And just as suddenly as it had obviously begun, round one of the big fish grab was over. And I was standing there with an empty dip net and an empty cooler, as usual about a day late and a dollar short.

Of course people are slow to obey an order like that. They had to waddle to their containers—Did I mention that a good many of these people were already fat?—and begin the slow trek of getting them up to solid ground, within reach of their vehicles. But a gradual movement toward a cease-fire of fishgrabbing was established, and all of us started to move in a more or less somewhat orderly fashion toward the stairs, some of us quite happier than others. Fish were still flopping out there behind us, by the hundreds, maybe by the thousands. It was all so big, it would have taken a long time to scour every pool to see what was still in it. My heart was heavy, and my hands reeked not. It was a long way up to the top, and

halfway there I had to do sort of a Good Samaritan
thing. These two old dudes who looked to be in their
seventies easily were trying to make their way to the
top with one of those tall garbage carts or cans on
wheels. It was stuffed full of fish. They couldn't see
much for all the sweat they couldn't keep mopped out
of their eyes, and the stringy muscles in their arms were
shining black ribbons of fatigue. And they were only
about a third of the way up. So shoot, I stopped, told the
one in front I'd spell him for a while if he'd hold on to
my friend's dip net and cooler and he did, quick. It was
pretty amazing to start lugging it up the sandbag stairs
and keep seeing what was coming up all around us, a
large wave of humanity, people of all shapes and sizes
and ages, all of them lugging at least a few fish, and
quite a few of them quite a lot of fish. When we got two
thirds of the way up I swapped places with the other old
guy and he got to hold the dip net and the cooler for a
while and the other old guy took his place back and we
finally hauled it up on level ground and they both
thanked me profusely and mopped at their faces some
more. I got Lorna's stuff back and went to find them
still over by the fence. Pretty soon it became apparent
that hope was running high among the crowd that a
second, later fish grab might take place once all the water in the last pool was pumped out. We stood around
and talked about the possibility of that for a while.

Some park ranger types descended into the rocks below to scoop up small catfish with fine mesh dip nets, and eventually these were passed out and taken away in buckets. Lorna and Paddy Chayovsky procured some in this manner.

After some more of that blistering heat we decided to go to their air-conditioned touring van for some cooler air and refreshments. I sat on the middle seat in the back and fixed a big Coke over ice and Lorna and Paddy Chayovsky had cheese sandwiches and drank cold beer and root beer in the front. It was hot enough to make a cow pee on a flat rock.

After a while I got back out and took a walk over to the lip of the spillway and leaned on the regular full-time fence there, the one that had steel posts sunk into the concrete and that heavy twisted wire. What I saw was a thing similar to a pod of whales or a murder of crows or a gaggle of geese: a cuddle of catfish weighing two to five pounds, hundreds of them, swimming around with their mouths out of the water in the pool the people had vacated, steadily sucking air. It was a little weakening, thinking about that water getting pulled down another foot or so and then wading in with a stringer in your hand. I had to go lie down under a tree for a little while, and when I got back up I edged slowly ooooooover the road over the spillway where I didn't know if I was supposed to go or not, because there were

some signs saying that maybe I wasn't supposed to be
over there, but all the construction workers and park
rangers were clustered around the crane talking and
gesturing and checking their watches, and it wasn't easy
at all to tell what was going on, and I knew that all
kinds of potential fishmongers like me, guys or gals
who'd missed the crucial first lightning grab, were probably coming up to them over and over and one by one
and saying something like, "So, dude, man, y'all gonna
let us git back down and dirty with those babies and
tickle em a little more, what you think, Bub?" and sure
enough they made an announcement that was amplified, said they were going to take an hour for lunch and
to "secure," whatever that meant, and then they'd be
back. They didn't say whether they were going to let us
back in after lunch or not. So I wandered on over to the
other side of the spillway, just taking a few steps at a
time in case anybody was watching me, not making
like I was headed straight over there at a hard walk or
anything. I just kind of meandered and looked up at the
sky once in a while and before I knew it I was over in
the other parking lot, the one that was just like the one
across the spillway except that it was totally empty.
I looked down. Those catfish babies, boy. I was right
on top of them. They were just about forty or fifty feet
down. But they were swimming around in there, and
their whiskers, you could see them, and their fins, and

they were all at least a couple of pounds and plenty of them were five pounds, and it looked like more and more of them by the minute were coming to the top to get air just like minnows in a bucket, which made sense. They'd had all that other water but all that other water was now gone. They didn't know what the hell had happened. They were just hanging out, eating crustaceans and insects and the occasional barbed worm, and their oxygen levels started dropping, and the water got shallower. So then they came to the top for air, and it was bright, and there was noise, and it was getting crowded, and there were all these legs and hands and feet . . .

I wanted those catfish. I wanted them. I didn't mind waiting around if they were going to let people go back in. I could probably wait a few hours if I had to. I could get in the shade if Lorna and Paddy Chayovsky wanted to get on home. But I'd already driven all the way down there, over little two-laned roads, crossing the Little Yocona a couple of times on a couple of different state highways. I'd seen red Chow dogs all morning. Almost everybody who lived between where I lived and where I was standing had a red Chow dog. One had been dead in the road with a warped grin on his face. The fish kept teeming below. I looked everything over some more and then wandered back to the van.

Lorna and Paddy had their own deal to go take care

of, putting the small catfish in a pond somewhere, and
they needed some sleep, too, so they decided to head toward the house. I thanked them and we said bye and
they left. After that I decided I'd walk back up to my
truck and get in it and drive it closer.

It was a hot walk back up there in my boots. I'd left
the truck under a little bitty pitiful tree that shaded just
a corner of one of the coolers, and when I got up there I
raised the lids on a couple of them and saw that my ice
was melting pretty fast. So I fixed another Coke and got
in and drove it back down to the kind of pavilion place
that you always have in a state park and parked it next
to one of those hummerjummers where you go in one
side by your gender and do your thing and we all know
that sometimes it can be a tad seedy in there with nasty
things written on the walls, but you only hope there are
not perverts lurking, some whacko whipping his mule
in one of the stalls.

I sat there for five minutes or so and then got out and
walked around and looked at everything and read a sign
about what kind of fish were in the lake with pictures
on them next to this roofed-over thing where there were
things kind of like sinks but probably more like em-
balmers' tables, long slanted stainless steel things where
I guess you dress your fish and just slide head guts scales
slime and all down this chute and maybe later, I don't
know, a park ranger carts it off somewhere.

I walked up under some trees and stood around under them for a while, probably looked like a dork with those hot boots on, and I walked along the edge of the people fence and saw how much effort it had taken to erect it, and then I watched some water come out of this long hose that was hooked up to the pump they'd been running off and on. It would run a little while and stop. Run a while and stop. Run a little and stop. It might spurt some. It might spurt some more. Then it'd stop. Then it'd run. Then it'd spurt. Then it'd stop. Then it'd run a little while. I got to playing this stupid guessing game with myself about how long it would be between spurts or runs or stops and wasted some time doing that, then finally went on back up under the shade.

Why in the hell didn't I just go back home?

Any fool could have seen that it was over, man.

Any fool but me.

What had happened, too, was that I'd gotten terrifically hungry. I hadn't had anything to eat in probably about sixteen hours or so, so there was a noise in my stomach like a small beaver that lived in there and wanted out, and he was gnawing, gnawing.

Lorna and Paddy Chayovsky had scored their cheese sandwiches from a store up the road, they'd said, so I got into my truck with a fresh Coke and my cap and Ray-Bans on and hung a cigarette from my lips and drove out of the little circular grove of shade trees and back up the hump of the road across the dam and alongside the lake with its bright boats and skiers towing their white fans of water, all of it pretty, serene, and actually mind-numbingly beautiful, that mix of water and wind and sun and fresh air, how good to be in old God's hands in green Mississippi.

I didn't know where the place was, but I took this fork. It seemed like they'd said something about going over this bridge. I went over this bridge. I looked down and it was I-55, Jackson to Memphis, cars and trucks whizzing, me just poking twenty-five above them, them going north and south, me going east and west, wheeeeeeeee!

I wanted ice and I had to have food. I had to stop at a stop sign on another road and let a few cars and trucks whiz by. Across the road I could see a store, and out front a man was down on his knees and he looked like he was cleaning out an ice machine.

I went on across and pulled into the parking lot, which was gray and hot. I nodded to the man and went on in. What happened next is still not entirely understandable to me. The inside of the store was made up to look like a store, and it had an overabundance of labeled goods in cans, things like sardines and potted meat and Vienna sausage and pork & beans, not just a few of them, and a great stock of Beanee Weenees as well. There were also bright jars of candy, and bright

polished walls, and things had little aprons on them,
but the people inside the store were the strangest of all.
They were older people, and the women had nice hair,
and smart blouses and shorts, and the men were dressed
in very clean overalls, and had flowing silver hair, and
they were all busy being polite to one another. If they
noticed that I had entered, they did not give any indica-
tion. And I began to feel truly weird. From the outside it
had looked like a regular country store.

I looked around for a sign that maybe advertised
sandwiches, and there was only a sign for pies. Pies. I
didn't want pies, maybe a slice with coffee after, sure,
but right then I wanted a sandwich I could sink my
teeth into, some bologna or cheese and bread with mustard or turkey slathered with mayonnaise would have
been good, just some *food* I could stuff in my *gut*, because my stomach was going *crazy*, saying all kinds of
things about how it would take anything, and a gentler
and more reasonable voice inside said No, no, go for a
sandwich, see about these strange people, see if they
know how to make a sandwich, and I looked at them,
and they seemed like caricatures of something they
were supposed to be, like downhome country folks, like
they belonged in a Cracker Barrel restaurant advertise-
ment, like they were just props or decoration, because
they just kept on being polite to each other, like there
was a script they were following that didn't include a

fishmonger like me, with rubber boots on, and they never even looked around at me, and so, disheartened and spooked, I backed out through the door, and the little bell above called after me, but none of them did.

Then I had to talk to the guy at the ice machine, who turned to me.

I nodded at it. "Outa ice, huh?"

He nodded kindly. "Yeah. Be bout a hour."

I nodded uproad. "Is there another store up here?"

He nodded unhappily back at his machine. "Yeah. Bout two miles."

I thanked him and got back into my dusty little brown Ram 50. The man who had put together the Mitsubishi motor might have had an uncle who had dive-bombed a Mitsubishi airplane at our boys in Pearl Harbor on that Sunday morning before church. They were probably waking up with hangovers from a big Saturday night in Hawaii. I knew there were worse ironies in the world. I aimed south, and pulled out into the road.

They were the longest two miles I ever drove. I kept looking and looking, and the store never showed up, and I kept driving, and it was brutal, and my feet were as hot as panting puppies in the boots. I had some flip-flops in the back for whenever I finally got them off my feet. I drove some more, and the landscape was hilly and dry and hot and baked and barren, and there was warm wind blowing through the truck, and the two Vivarin I'd taken a long time before then had completely stopped doing their thing. There wasn't anybody I knew back over there, and the smart thing to do was just turn around and go home, and fix something to eat there, and then turn on the air in my dark bedroom and get into the bed and sleep until whenever I was ready to get up and resume my life. But greediness had raised its whiskered head in me. If they gave some more fish away and I had plenty of ice, they might let me take all I wanted. They might get that crane to working and send people down in there to put the fish in barrels and bring them up. That pump was down there for a reason. Somebody had spent some time and had maybe risked danger and had certainly gone to a hell of a lot of trouble getting that thing down in there, and that could only mean that they were going to pump it totally dry to do the spillway inspection, and that meant all the fish would have to come out. That was the way I saw it. That was probably one of the main reasons that crane was sitting there, to put that pump down in there, and then lift the rest of the remaining fish out once the General Public had made their grab, and then lift the pump out. So it made sense to me that if I stuck around, I might still get some fish out of the deal. There wouldn't be any question about dressing them before sleep, but I could probably get enough ice on them to make sure they'd be okay until after I got some rest.

The road went over hills and more hills and some more hills and then one flattened out and there was a long low building on the left, some signs out front, gas pumps that were old. I made sure a truck with my number on it wasn't coming toward me or up behind me and pulled safely off over there and parked. It looked like a good place in that it looked like it had been there for a while. It was made of brown wood, and it had a tin roof, and it advertised fishing gear for sale, and there were cane poles in stands, and bread signs, and it must have been in Grenada County because they had cold beer signs. Out front were also some empty wooden stalls like they might sell vegetables when vegetables are in season.

Somebody came out and waved and got into his pickup and cranked it and pulled away. I went in. It was like a lot of country stores these days. It had suffered the same sad fate. It had tried to go deli. Some guy was behind the counter, but he was partially hidden by a bunch of racks of potato chips and cardboard displays of different things, air fresheners for your car, nail clippers, hair nets, packs of snelled hooks, all kinds of things. Near the back I spied the minnow tank and dip nets and lures and corks and other accouterments of the fisherman's life, and there was a big meat case with the now-familiar rounds of meat and cheese they can slice slices from, so my eyes went to a sandwich board and saw a straight-up bologna sandwich for a buck fifty. They had little snack cakes, all that, short rows of canned food but not as much as the place I'd just left. The guy might have put on an apron but I'm not sure. But he came back there and asked if he could help me and I took a good look at the guy and ordered a plain bologna on white with mustard, and then thought about it and got him to add a piece of cheese.

> **RIFF:** It was kind of strange, me ordering that sandwich made that way, because usually when I eat a bologna sandwich I don't put cheese on it unless I'm going to microwave it, and I used to do that when I worked in a stove factory, about ten times a week for about a year, but it's probably been two or three years now since I've fixed one that way. It melts the cheese good, all right, but sticking it in that microwave does something to it and makes the bread tough and, if you can believe this, the sandwich unsatisfying to eat.

All I can remember about the guy is that he was kind of reddish: reddish hair, kind of a reddish shirt, reddish fur on his arms. His hair was greased back with Vitalis or something equally slick, and he resembled David Caruso vaguely. I said something about the big fish grab and needing some more ice, and I asked him if he had

any. I wanted plenty for all the fish I was going to get after the park ranger people came back from lunch. Sometime soon after entering the store and realizing that I
was going to get some food, I'd probably made a then-
unconscious decision to just tough it on out to the bitter end, knowing that I could always eventually sleep
whenever all this was over.

It amused him to no end that I'd been down to the big
fish grab.

"Boy, a shitload of folks show up for that!" he
shouted. "Every time it's the same thing! A shitload of
folks shows up! Those park guys try to keep it quiet, but
they can't keep it quiet!" he shouted. He worked on my
sandwich for a few seconds and then shouted, "Hah! I
didn't even know myself they was doing it again! They
musta kept it good and quiet this time!"

I told him I'd heard about it in Oxford, which was
thirty miles away. He went on making my sandwich.
Taped to the meat case were Polaroid pictures of people
holding monster catfish, monster bass, monster bream,
monster crappie. You could have fished every day for the
rest of your life with all the fishing gear they had in that
store and still willed some to your grandsons.

My new friend kept a running line of giggling and
babbling going back there about past fish grabs he'd witnessed. I spied some pickled eggs and big dill pickles on
top of the meat case and told him I needed two eggs and

one pickle. He wrapped my sandwich in waxed paper and slid a toothpick through the center of it and with tongs reached out my pickle and eggs, put them on waxed paper, too. I paid up front for the food and five more bags of ice and some smokes and at the last second I snagged a bag of Lay's barbecued potato chips.

I ate going down the road, back through the dusty hills, and it was even worse almost except it didn't seem to take as long to get back. All my stuff was in the seat, the torn-open bag of potato chips, the sandwich on its waxed paper, the eggs and pickle on theirs, and some open packs of pepper and salt I'd used, and some napkins he'd put in the sack, and the sack, and all the tapes that I can never keep straight as to where a particular one is at any given time, whether Alejandro Escovedo is in the truck or Marlana Antonia's car or Louisa Latigo's car or the coolpad or the dining room or the bedroom or over at the shack. And there was some other junk on the floor, my cutting heads for my Stihl cutter, and a chain saw wrench, and some extra blades for a grass head, and some empty coffee cups, and finally, a bunch of Coke cans. I felt like a man who was about to be hanged. An uneasy feeling in the pit of my stomach along with a feeling of abandon that was not quite reckless. Some funky radio station was on out of Memphis, fading in and out, playing lousy songs and doing too many commercials, talking about the heat, so I put on a tape that somebody had made for me and sent to me, one that had various artists. I'd listened to it so much I was about sick of it, you know how you get. Something that starts out so wonderful doesn't stand the test of time and miles on the road, and you have to find something new, but I was sick of everything I had in the truck, I thought, and it was a dangerous thing to be doing, to be looking through all your tapes and lunch waxed papers when you're already driving and eating at the same time and half-crazed with sleep deprivation.

I turned again at the faux country store and went back across I-55 again, munching my bologna and taking brief pity on those driving so fast below, rushing to wherever they were going. The eggs were way too bitter from having been in the jar so long, and the pickle was about as crunchy as a hot noodle. The bread stuck to the top of my dry mouth.

Some of the construction folks were back, along with the park ranger folks, but it was plain that some sort of tide had been turned. There were hardly any vestiges left of the throbbing mass of humanity that had been there a mere two hours before. A few hopefuls hung in the fence still, and I took another bite of my sandwich as I drove around the curve of the road to park near the pavilion thing. I couldn't stand it any longer. I got out the flip-flops and left my lunch in the truck, hobbled into the shade and sat down to take the boots off and just breathe a big long sigh of relief when those dogs hit that cooler air. I think I actually said aloud, "Awwwwwwwwwwwwwwwwwyeah."

I beat feet back to the truck for the rest of my food and spread everything out on a park table to finish it. I knew that Paddy Chayovsky and Lorna were fast asleep, heads probably tousled with slumber under the quiet roar of a BTU blast of frigid air. And even if I left now I would never understand what the hell I had done or why I had done it.

Oh boy. How these things happen. You get involved and the time just gets away. I could have at least been home sleeping in preparation for work, it wasn't like I hadn't done any work, I had, quite a bit of it, for unbroken months at a time, some of it in bedrooms, some of it in dining rooms, some of it in cold-water-only motels at Sardis where they don't have any coffee in the lobby and you can forget about buying any food in town after ten P.M., oh no, not in Sardis. You have to go down darkened I-55 South into darkened North Batesville, where it looks like you'd stand a good chance of getting mugged, to get old chicken that's been in the warmer too long, all day, probably, so it wasn't like I'd just been enjoying a festive picnic all summer.

Nobody knew anything solid on our side of the fence, but the air was rife with rumors. I talked to some people who were hanging around one of the fish-dressing stations, and somebody had told some of them that the park ranger dudes had told them that they were going to put some people down in the hole when the water got pumped out some more, and then send barrels down on a platform with the crane, and then haul the fish in the barrels up when the people down in the hole got through loading them. But that rumor had a double edge: They also said that they weren't going to give any more of the fish away, that they were going to put them in a dump truck and take them to some farmers' fields and dump them on the ground for fertilizer. This seemed a pretty stunning revelation to me. I knew there were at least a couple of hundred good eating-size catfish in that pool. And there were plenty of people like me standing around, people who would eat them, given half a chance to go after them. But a man must not beg for his fish.

I didn't know how much longer I could stand up. My food hadn't settled on my stomach very well and I was having some gas from it already and a morbid rising gaseous bubble had lodged in my throat just somewhere south of my esophagus, felt like, and it wouldn't come loose.

I don't know how much longer I stood there, hoping against hope. I saw steel garbage cans loaded onto a flat skid and hoisted into the air, then lowered out past the fence and into the bottom of the pool. They'd told people to stay back now. The time for close viewing of what was going on down within those concrete walls was over. The clamps of government had clamped down. Messing with these people was messing with the U.S. Army. One park ranger dude in helmet and crisp uniform came by on the inside of the fence, the hangers-on like me assailing him with hands palm up for free fish like blind folks panhandling alms, but he never stopped walking long enough to hold a conversation with anybody, only saying to the crowd in general as he went along that we all knew that if he wasn't going to get any, then none of us were.

It was bitter news to take. That was when I began to feel that the vise was closing, and that decisions had already been made, and that some official function was taking place, and that we weren't all just good sharing neighbors anymore, and that there were two sides to this thing now, them on that side of the fence, us on this one.

But surely there were children connected with all these people who could eat some of the fish, and probably some old people, too, and I just couldn't understand the logic of dumping perfectly good food on the ground that somebody could take home, and clean, and cook, and eat, and enjoy. Even if I couldn't get any, I who already had some fish in the freezer, and could always go catch some more, why not give the rest of the edible ones to somebody who could use them? What the hell did our tax dollars go for if they couldn't at least feed some people who would be glad of it? Was this America or was it not?

I stood around awhile longer, until I saw the guy who'd been smoking cigarettes in the cab of the crane turn back around in his seat and start operating the levers again. The cables tightened and they moved out there and the skid full of barrels came back up, and a lone worker went over there once the crane operator had set it down, and he hooked some more cables to it and then got on it, and stood on it with the barrels as a dirty white dump truck came rolling in and stopped in a tiny cloud of dust. The worker and the fish went up, and hovered over the dump truck, and the worker took hold of the barrels one at a time and emptied them into the truck. The fish slid out, the slick with the scaly, mostly the fabled whisker kitten. Each barrel had about fifty gallons of fish and there were six of them. Three hundred gallons of fish going to hell without a handbasket.

Hope died there then among us. You could feel it seep out and float away somewhere. Even in shock I witnessed a weird dog, a retired greyhound, I think, very strangely shaped and with assorted hair. The catfish were slapping wetly down into the dump truck. The worker finished what he was doing, and gave a signal to the crane operator, who set him down, where he got off. The skid with the barrels rose into the air again, and descended into the concrete chasm again, and I imagined a hot Yalobusha or Grenada County soybean field late that afternoon, and the piles of fish starting to pale in the sun, and of how the flies would come, and then the crows, and the buzzards, and the possums, and then the coons, and I knew that the owls would watch silently from the trees that night while it became a thing a person wouldn't want to look at.

The last of us started to drift apart. We gave little waves, no names known, none needed. A few warriors had been bloodied, not all who had sought it, but a great sack had been made. All over Yalobusha and Grenada Counties there would be fish frying on stoves that night. It would be a thing a child would remember as an old grayed woman, the radio going in the kitchen and the black-iron skillets, the crispness of a perfect hush puppy, the delicate crunch of a meal-coated fin.

My old truck was sitting there in the hot sun, itself a badly beaten but still able warrior. I knew it would gladly take me back home, to rest in the shade of the house Howard made. I got my tired ass into it and it cheerfully cranked. I pulled out, knowing those Mitsubishi airplanes probably ran like a son of a bitch. Like a wild-ass ape. The road was windy and hot and sunny, and the red Chows had all sought the succor of shade from the day. A little later, when I passed by Lorna and Paddy Chayovsky's, I beeped the little tinny horn, just to let them know, if they were awake and looking out the window, where I was at that moment in the world.

The Whore in Me

AFTER WHAT SEEMS like a few minutes, the phone rings in your darkened room. You answer it. It's Craig. He works for your publisher. He wants you to meet him in the lobby in ten minutes.

There's no time to shower, no time to do anything but brush your teeth and pull on the clothes you took off last night. As you dress in groaning misery you remember walking around looking for your room after you left the lounge, thinking you were in room 116, when actually you are in 216, but that didn't stop you from trying to get in 116 with your little card, over and over. You might have terrified some innocent person. Finally you went back to the front desk and got the night manager to take you to your room personally. You hated to do it, but that's what they get paid for. She found it for you, and got you in there, and then you slept the sleep of the long dead. There were no dreams of any kind.

You know you probably present a very sorry spectacle

walking up to Craig and Janet. You know your eyes are red and you've lost your Visine somewhere on the road. The road eats up a lot of things but that is the nature of the road. Craig and Janet are nice and they get you into the car and you're glad somebody is there to take care of you since it seems you aren't capable of taking care of yourself.

At the convention center you get coffee, a few cigarettes, and begin to wake up. The breakfast doesn't start until eight so you wander next door to the gun show and check out some 1850 flintlock rifles, some blackpowder pistols even older than that. They've got some really cool shit. Old knives. Swords. You think about hiding out there for a while, posing as somebody else. But after a while you have to go back to the book business and get your scrambled rubbery eggs, some juice, a biscuit, more coffee. You eat quickly, then go back to the lobby for that last cigarette. You are barely able to move, yet you have to give a reading. It feels like the beginning of a very bad day.

You read. You talk to people. You sign books. You hang out in the booth. About noon, Janet, an angel of mercy, gives you the keys to her car and you go out there in the hot parking lot, roll the windows down, take off your murderous boots and your wool coat and try to sleep in the backseat, but it's cramped and small and impossible. After a while you get back up.

In another hour or so they take you back to the airport. You stand outside and smoke a cigarette. You won't get another one until you leave the Los Angeles airport some six hours from now. But you'll be in Mark's Cadillac at that point, and everything should be an extremity of cool.

You fly and you fly and you fly and you fly. Before flying you waited and you waited and you waited and you waited some more. There was no food, not because it wasn't available, but because you didn't want any. You didn't drink anything. You didn't feel very good. As a matter of fact you felt pretty fucking rotten.

Coming into L.A. you can't believe again how big it is. You think you may have to have a cheeseburger.

Mark is waiting in baggage claim with his back to you but you recognize his black cap, his black hair, his black coat, and he gives you that big crooked grin you know so well, and then you've got your luggage and are in his large car and moving down the road.

You stop and eat in Redondo Beach, have a drink, talk shop. It's a good meal, catfish in L.A. Later you go out to his house in Rancho Palos Verdes and then Jennifer comes in and you hug her. About midnight you go to bed, grateful to be where you are, finally, among friends so valued and good.

Sunday is a day of rest. They go to church, you sleep late, have coffee, read the papers. In the afternoon you drive over to the supermarket and get those fat boy T-bone steaks.

Late that evening you mix a couple of Bloody Marys and climb with Mark to the high hill behind his house, walking fat boy Ray, who is half Beagle, half Rottweiler, whom you once kept for a couple of weeks at your house in Mississippi, while Mark and Jennifer were taking a Christmas trip. Ray remembers you, and it's good to see him again, too.

The land rises steeply around you and the view of the ocean and the other hills is magnificent. You just sit and look at it all. Mark says that sometimes they see whales. There are peacocks, sixty to seventy of them, running loose. This land, outside the city, is awesome and spectacular. You don't see any of this on *L.A. Law*. After a long while you go back down to the house with him.

That night you cook the steaks and they are tender, medium rare, delicious. After supper you have a few drinks on the patio with him and then you go to bed, pleasantly worn out. Actually exhausted. Your legs are sore from walking around hotels lost and your feet still hurt. But finally you have come to a place on the book tour where you can rest with a brother in what you do.

◆ ◆ ◆

VAGABOND BOOKS IN Brentwood is packed with people Monday night. You spend two and a half hours in the bookstore and you sign many many books, new ones as well as old ones. You spent the day taking it easy on the patio, sipping coffee, listening to Leon Russell and k.d. lang, feeling the tiredness ease out of your bones, and the knot in your stomach slowly loosening, thinking of what all you've left behind you, the flights, the people in the stores, the bad food, the books, the drinks, the walking. You know that the rest of it's going to be a piece of cake. You cooked eggs and sausage for you and Mark today.

Craig Graham owns Vagabond and you haven't seen him in five years, but you once met John O'Brien in his old store, long before *Leaving Las Vegas* was a movie, long before John took his own life. You speak of him with Craig. You're beginning to segue a bit now, you're beginning to be a little bit glad now that you are on tour. You're glad to be where you are now.

People keep coming up, over and over. Craig furnishes beer in green bottles and you're signing books and drinking beer. Craig is so glad to see you that he tells you you can even smoke in the store, but when you take a short break after your reading, you smoke in the parking lot out back simply out of respect for the bookstore.

L.A. is suffused in darkness now and just up the

street is Nicole Brown Simpson's house, the scene of the infamous crime. You go back inside and finish up with the books, and Craig says that people have been calling all day. It's a good thing to hear, and you head across the street to the Daily Diner for a hamburger steak with onions. You can't smoke in there, either, but they make a good Margarita. Later on, midway through your meal, you order a Wild Turkey and Coke, but they seem uncertain how to make it, or maybe the little blond beach girl waitress just can't understand your homeboy accent. What she brings back is a glass filled with ice and Coke, and another glass filled with ice and Wild Turkey. But you don't mind. Today has been a very good day, and Sunday wasn't bad either. You, like Merle Haggard, are glad you've got a friend in California.

TALKING TO MARK is one of the best things about being out here, sharing ideas, sharing secrets, talking about plans and work, and how we're always up for whatever gig brings in the dough. How you work your ass off and it's a big old groaning bear that won't get off and can't get off because there's no way for it to get off. Everything else has to fall by the wayside: family, friends, social engagements other than those that take place by yourself on a black dirt road in a moving truck and a little Leonard Cohen. When your bros don't see you in the bar for three months they know you're working. One day months later you show up and they slap you on the back and ask you how it's going. You smile sadly and say: It's over. And riding in the long brown Caddy is good, too. You rode in it some in Mississippi. We tell jokes in there, chuckle up some anecdotes, cruising up and down the California coast like a couple of L.A. lowriders, which, for now, is exactly what we are.

You get up late on Tuesday and have coffee, cigarettes, a few Fig Newtons. Your feet are better now that you've had your boots off so much. Mark makes tuna fish sandwiches on dark bread and he puts on lettuce and mixes in olives and cucumbers. He shares with you a big bag of Ruffles. You take a shower and a nap and get ready for Book Soup. One more bookstore and Wednesday you go home. You'll do Oxford, you'll do Nashville, and a few days later New York. You'll wind up in Texas, in Washington state, in Iowa and Minnesota, North Carolina and Miami, and lots of other places, and it will be a long haul until November.

But things seem to be smoothing out now. You grab a beer from Mark's refrigerator, and the two of you head down the hill to the car. Your time with him is almost over.

Now you're on the plane back to Chicago, two hours late, and there's a sense of dread inside you that you won't get home tonight. Mark took you to the airport this morning, after a good crowd at Book Soup last night. You had a couple of beers and some schnapps, and saw some friends from Mississippi, and Buck Henry sitting at a table near the door. Mark talked you out of giving him a high five. You had supper in a good restaurant with some movie folks you're working for, and Elizabeth of Taylor, Mississippi, who had just arrived. Now, hopefully, you're on your way home. Tomorrow night you'll do the store at home, and Blue Mountain will play, and the entire bookstore will be filled with your friends. It will be good to be home. But already you miss your big black-haired friend.

You don't make it home this night. Something was wrong with the plane and they had to fix it, so you spent the night in Chicago. Your wife had driven an hour and a half to Memphis to pick you up, and then you weren't there. There was nothing to do but catch another plane the next morning, in the rain of Chicago, and wait for it to land you back in Tennessee.

YOU'RE HOME NOW. All your friends are in Square Books, and Blue Mountain is playing, and there is a long line of people for whom you sign books. They're serving beer and all your children are here and your wife is here and your mother is here beside you. You don't feel like much of a whore anymore, now that you're among your own people. It's not over yet, and you've still got to drive to Nashville tomorrow night, but it's a lot better than what it was. You can rest now, and sleep in your own bed, and play with your dogs. Part of it is over, not all of it, but you know that one day it will all be over, and you can return to your unremarkable life, the one where you sit every day at this machine and write your little words, and drink your coffee, and wander out in the yard.

For now, the rest of the road waits.

Goatsongs

SAW THE SON of a bitch while I was up on my tractor, running the rotary cutter along a wall of green
sagegrass that was five feet high. It was August, hot,
on over in the afternoon but not near sundown. The sky
had softened, and the coyote was trotting along in the
open like the most unconcerned thing you could imagine. I stopped the tractor when I realized that he hadn't
seen me. Or maybe hadn't registered what I was.

He ambled on across the freshly clipped pasture grass
I'd cut the week before and dropped over into a patch of
stuff about two feet high and stopped. I cut back on the
throttle and the Cummins diesel sat there doing its
steady chug. I knocked it into neutral and took the PTO
out of gear, and heard the swigswigswig of the six-foot
blade slowing down a little, turning freely, but so heavy
and with so much momentum going that it would take
it close to two minutes to finally come to a complete

stop. He laid himself down in the grass and I got off the tractor.

Just for the fun of it, I thought, I wonder how close you could get to him if you kept the outline of the tractor behind you and walked in a straight line to him. I didn't have a gun. It was in the cabinet with the others at the house, and the house was about a quarter mile across the pasture. I could see it, cars and trucks parked in front of it. I couldn't hear anything because of the tractor running. It would sit there and run like a clock as long as fuel was going to the motor. I didn't think I'd be able to get close to him. But I hated him so bad I wanted to get another look at him. I wanted to kill him was what I wanted to do. But the gun was too far away. He'd probably run before I took many steps. But I started taking some anyway.

The glimpse I'd had of him, he didn't look all coyote. He looked about half dog, or coy-dog. He looked like about half malamute, because he had patches of tan and black, and his ears didn't look right. I knew it happened. I knew they bred with dogs sometimes and I knew that they ate a lot of dogs, and I knew they ate baby goats, too. I knew that bitterly, and I wished hard for my gun in my hand with each step I took. I took a surprising number of them in a straight line and he didn't get up and run. I couldn't see him, but my eyes had never left the spot where he'd stopped, even when I was climbing down from the tractor, so unless he'd crawled away, he was still there.

The distance closed from fifty yards to forty to thirty to twenty, and once I got away from the tractor it didn't make very much noise, like the land absorbed it somehow, or maybe the tall patch of grass I'd been mowing was muffling the sound. I wouldn't have thought he'd have just trotted out across the open like that with me up on the tractor, but since I wasn't walking on two legs it messed him up somehow, let him get within shooting distance of a man, a man who, luckily for the coyote, had no gun.

I knew he was still there and I wondered what he would do if I surprised him. Would he run? If surprised at close quarters would he come at me? I didn't have anything but a pocketknife, but I took it out and opened it up. I started taking baby steps then, looking into that tall grass, and when I got to within twenty feet or so I could see a brown mottled form curled and at rest, just a vague glimpse of it through the grass while the wind swayed it, and I figured he was taking a nap. And reckon how long he'd sleep? Reckon he'd sleep long enough for me to back all the way back to the tractor and get on the other side of it and then run bent over behind the wall of sagegrass back to the house and get the single-barrel out of the cabinet, and some buckshot, and then run back? And do this whole sneaking-up thing again until I got close enough for just one damn shot? Just one.

There wasn't anything to do but try. I started backing up, real slowly, real careful, watching the spot where he was.

As FAR AS I could tell, the Immaculate Kid came one afternoon when we least suspected him. We never even expected him. I was just driving the tractor around one afternoon, drove by Nanette lying in some grass and there was a little white thing with black spots next to her. You'd have thought I'd gone crazy. I started blowing the horn on the tractor, and whooping and hollering, and they heard me over there in the yard and came over, and I showed them our first baby goat.

This was before bestial incest crept into the picture.

What happened was that we'd taken Nanette on for a while. Tom had been trying to keep her in his pasture in town and it just wasn't working out. But we have sixty-two acres out here, or my wife and her mama do, and they let me live on it, and Billy Ray raises cows on it.

Billy Ray had gone to the sale at Pontotoc one Saturday. That's one of those big barn deals where they run livestock into the ring, cows, pigs, bulls, heifers, horses and mules, donkeys and burros sometimes, and they've got an auctioneer with a microphone and he's sitting up there in a booth above the smoke and the sawdust in the ring and once in a while a young pig jumps through the steel pipe ring and maybe shits in somebody's lap. You can sell or buy. Billy Ray bought what he thought was a young goat that turned out to be a pygmy goat full grown. He had Tom's permission to breed Nanette. But when he got that hairy thing home I said, Forget it, man, he ain't going to be able to get up on her. Nanette was a regular-size-goat. We watched him try. She'd just be grazing while he was hunching on her. So we said, Nah, ain't gonna work, and Billy Ray sold the pygmy goat to somebody else and I forgot all about it until that afternoon I found the Immaculate Kid. We called a couple of friends of ours and said, Oh hey come over and look at the cute baby goat. They came over, we took pictures, made videos, and Joe even got down behind an overturned feed trough with a pig puppet on his hand and messed with the little goat's head and we had a big time. The pygmy goat had been gone for a long time, we thought way too long to have impregnated Nanette some way and left her alone all this time and her still deliver a baby. We were glad about it. We celebrated the young goat's life, such as we could. We just didn't know then all the trouble that lay down the road waiting for us. Because when you start messing with goats, well, they're not cows. They're goats, and somehow they achieve a realm of even worse nastiness than do cows. It's probably pretty hard to believe unless you've witnessed it yourself. But it does occur. I told Billy Ray. He wouldn't listen to me. Even when the baby goats started getting killed at night later. Even when they started getting their throats slashed. That's always the problem: He won't listen to me.

But, he's tough as hell, can go out and work in all kinds of bad weather, and is already a much better man than I ever thought about being, except that he thinks women ought to stay in their own place. But he's real smart and funny, and he's already twenty-four, and it's only now, at forty-eight, that I can see how much of a boy I was at his birth, when I was twenty-four.

The Immaculate Kid never was good for much. He was too wild to pet, so we didn't get to play with him. After a while we just ignored him, and he and Nanette ranged over the pasture like the cows did, not really soulmates.

Billy Ray's got all kinds of cows, calves, heifers, bulls. Mamaw's place is sixty-two acres of good land with grass. And after the new goat had been hanging around for about six months, I began to wonder when those things became sexually active. And would a goat do its mother? I knew dogs would. I knew dogs would in a second. I don't figure big cats would do it. I think their family ties are stronger than that. But he didn't know and I didn't, but I went ahead and said something, you know, something like, Well look Bud, now, you don't want to

let that thing get old enough to where it'd get to thinking about screwing his mama before you sell him,
okay? And of course he assured me that wouldn't happen. And I went happily on with whatever project I was
involved in, either writing something or building something or cutting something down and dragging it somewhere I'm sure.

And one day I saw him riding her. A goat on its
mother. I found Billy Ray and said, Come on, let's get
him loaded up and sell him, we don't want to have baby
goats born from a mother and son, come on, go catch
him, and he did get up and try. He tried for a long, long
time. He chased that damn goat all over this place several times, and I don't remember how long it took him
to catch him, but I think it was a long time. Eventually
the goat got gone and I hoped Nanette wasn't pregnant.

Fast forward about three months and one morning
Nanette's got three babies about the size of rabbits, with
little striped faces and hanging ears, and they're bounc-
ing and bucking around on their new legs, and they were
just about the cutest things I'd ever seen in my life. One
was a black one, one was a little brown one, and one was
gray-and-black. You could pet them. They weren't de-
formed. They looked pretty normal. I felt a failure to
prevent animal incest nonetheless.

But they were just cute as hell. I got them into the
heifer pen because I was already thinking about coyotes.

The heifer pen's built out of woven wire and it's right behind Mamaw's house, where Babe, Billy Ray's big Walker hound, sleeps. I figured they'd be safer there. They weren't too hard to catch. They'd run, but you could catch them, and they'd bleat, maybe in terror, who knew? But eventually you could run them down and play with them some. I did it several times.

I MADE IT BACK to the tractor without him getting up and seeing me. I ducked behind it and bent over and started running. The wall of green sagegrass was a couple of hundred yards long. It's one of the main pastures and it grows so much grass the cows can't eat it all, so we have to mow it a few times each summer. That was what I'd been doing that afternoon. I'd mowed a lot of it but there was still plenty to go. It's probably six or seven acres, maybe more. It's hard for me to look at a piece of land and say how many acres are in it.

So there I was, running, bent over. Running bent over, running bent over, running bent over. It's a hard way to run. Man was not meant to run that way. I figured once I got a little ways off from him I could straighten up. But I wasn't going to stop running, not if I had even a slim chance of getting the gun and some shells and getting back up there before he left. I was going to shoot him in the head after what he'd done to my baby goats. He'd done come on the place and killed.

Over and over. I had the right to defend my livestock.
Even if they were all already dead.

So, I ran bent over for a long time, until I got down
under the slight rise of land that lay between us, and
then I straightened up and kept jogging back toward the
house.

I don't remember who was in there. I jogged to the
gun cabinet and got my Harrington & Richardson
single-shot 12-gauge, and scooped up some OO buckshot and some no. 4 steel shot and jogged back out the
door, shells in the pocket, piece at port arms. Like in
the bad old days of the marines when you'd get to do
that shit for nine miles. With a raincoat on. And a full
marching pack. Just because some sadistic son of a
bitch who outranked you was having a bad day. Or,
maybe, I don't know, he probably enjoyed doing it to us.
I know there are people like that.

MY DADDY HAD a goat one time, when he was
a little boy. He told me the story more than once. I can
imagine Tula back then, back in the thirties, the roads
dirt, my daddy with his little goat cart and the goat
pulling him down to the store. Thinking about him and
his goat gets me confused with the Faulkner story about
Boon Hogganbeck hitching a wild horse to a cart and it
knocking one of the wheels off on a post. But Daddy
told me about his little goat and how it would pull him

around everywhere, and how he kept it for a long time, and how one day finally they evidently decided to kill it and eat it and they cut its head off in front of him, and of how it kept on bleating even after they had cut its head off. Who would do some shit like that to a kid? Who did it? He never made that part clear.

THE LITTLE GOATS prospered and grew. Young children were brought out from Oxford to pet them and play with them. They made you just feel good in your heart, by God, to look out there in the heifer pen and see them prancing around, like they had springs under their feet, or all four legs were pogo sticks. They seemed to have limitless energy and enthusiasm. Nanette had a big old bag with fat teats winking from between her legs, and I even thought of milking her but never did.

The little goats got to be the size of big rabbits pretty soon. Their little bleats were musical, and Nanette seemed content. She was bad about butting, and Tom's youngest boy had gotten scared of her for that reason, but it never bothered me. Even if she hit you it wasn't that bad. If she hit me I'd just get ahold of her horns and wrestle with her for a while. She wasn't mean. She was just a goat.

I COULDN'T EVEN hear the tractor running at all. I said, Shit, it's done quit, and it's sitting there with

the key on, what's that going to do to it, anything? Will
it cause something to short out, some other stuff's already shorted out, it doesn't have any headlights or a
fuel gauge or a temperature gauge that works, what else
is going to go wrong with it?

I was still running and I knew there wasn't any
chance of him still being there by the time I got back.
Just more wasted effort, just one more thing you spend
time doing that doesn't pay off, what difference would
it make anyway, they're dead already, they're gone, but
in a bad way that lives within me I would have felt
better if I could have killed him. No solid proof that
he was the one, but he was the only one available and he
would do.

When I got back to the wall of sagegrass I bent over
again, and soon running running running I could hear
the short muffled murmur of the tractor still chugging,
odd how that distance swallowed all the sound up, but
nothing had changed up there. I stopped behind the
tractor and broke the shotgun open and pulled out some
shells. The no. 4 pellets were smaller but there were
more of them. I loaded the chamber and closed the gun
and went out front again. I knew he was gone. It had
been probably over ten minutes and he wouldn't have
lain there for that long, probably. Although with a wild
thing you wonder just how they do live, on winter
nights when the moon is up and ice hangs from all the

trees, and the grass is white and frosted and stiff. What warmth is there for them and where do they hide? But man has a tough time of it, too. He tries to raise goats for the joy their companionship brings. For the goat-songs they sing.

ME AND THE little goats never did exactly get to be best friends. I liked them fine, but it didn't seem to go the other way. They weren't like dogs, puppies, cats, kittens. They didn't live in the house or even on the front porch, although one time I took one of them over to the patio where the family was cooking out. It didn't really want to go, but I took my belt off and made a loop with the buckle and put the loop around its neck and opened the gate and started leading it out. Nanette got upset. She came after us. The little goat was bleating for her and she started bleating back and it just made the little one bleat harder and before long it started sounding like somebody was murdering them. But I closed the gate and took on off across Mamaw's yard with it, it kicking and struggling, trying to pull away, and I kept talking to it, and trying to pet it, but it didn't want to calm down, and it took a while to get it over on the patio. And it didn't like it over there, and kept on bleating, and although everybody thought it was cute, it was pretty obvious that it wasn't going to make much of a pet. I took it back to the pen and put it up. Billy Ray came home that evening and opened the gate and let them out in the pasture for some reason. The next morning there were only two baby goats.

BILLY RAY AND I have these little talks sometimes. I tell him how things are going to go if he doesn't do A or B and leave it at that and then when he doesn't do A or B it happens and we have to talk again. And I knew that I had made it perfectly clear to him that Nanette and her babies needed to stay in the heifer pen because of all the coyotes that were around. We'd shot them. We'd captured them. They were still here. Now we'd lost a baby goat because he hadn't listened to me. I told him, Let's get them back in the pen and let's keep them in there, okay? He said okay.

I got on the tractor while he herded them up back toward the heifer pen. I was holding out for hope, hoping against hope, hoping that maybe one of them had just gotten separated from her and was wandering around out in the pasture, bleating for her. But I made a wide and close sweep right before sundown and there was nothing. Meat, bones, blood. All gone. But like I said, it wasn't much bigger than a rabbit.

I COULDN'T TELL if he was gone or not. Everything looked the same. The tractor was still running. The wind was still blowing. There were some pieces of rusted tin lying out across the short pasture grass in front, remnants of the tornado of '84 that sucked the two-story barn up howling and spewed it back into thousands of pieces, and it was still lying here and there. Once in a while you'd run over a piece of it.

I had my shotgun up, ready to aim it. But I didn't see a damn thing to aim it at. I knew I couldn't be that lucky. I knew he was gone.

The place was green and beautiful. The sycamores that lined the creek were in full foliage and up past the other pond you could see the line of cedars along the fence. More than once I'd mowed a big patch of pasture and kept cutting it into ever smaller circles and seen the rats running, and then watched the hawks fall on them and carry them to the big oaks down in the bottom below the house and eat them perched on a limb, ruffling their feathers just before sundown. In long years past I'd fed Mary Annie's daddy's cows out of his blue-and-white '67 Chevy pickup, delivered their babies, hauled off the dead carcasses of some that hadn't made it. I'd been on this place over twenty years, had seen it change through weathers and wind and snow, had mowed it, fenced it, farmed it, made love and made children from that love on it. I didn't like anything coming on it and taking what he wanted.

◆ ◆ ◆

LIFE ROCKED ON. It always does. No matter what happens, you just keep going to the day you can't go anymore. I was saddened by the death of one of the little goats, even though I hadn't known it very personally, but I was determined that it wouldn't happen again. But Billy Ray has problems. He has cows and heifers and bulls and sometimes I don't fully understand every little increment of what's going down because I don't have time to listen to all of it, but I do sit down at night with him sometimes and discuss this cow or that cow. This fence or that fence. This bull or that bull. I know I will never be free of cows. And I know that's what he's interested in, even though I'm not, so I try to go along with him some and cheer him along some, although I know already the heartbreak of cow ownership and do not want to sip the wine of its fruits anymore in this life. He let the goats out again for some reason or another, and another one disappeared.

I got pretty pissed off then. I got the remaining two back in the heifer pen and I kept them in there. But one night not long after that, he came back again. The dogs raised a commotion, some bleating was heard, and the next morning when I went out Nanette was sitting very still with her horns caught in the woven wire and the last remaining little baby goat was lying close to the back gate with its throat torn open. It was quite dead. The son of a bitch didn't get to eat it, but he killed it anyway.

The way I saw it, I had failed as a livestock caretaker to take care of the stock entrusted to me. I don't think it bothered anybody else as much as it did me. I just couldn't quite reconcile it. It didn't seem fair.

Billy Ray had to haul the last baby goat off. I don't know where he took it. I'm sure wherever he took it, some coyotes found it and ate it anyway.

IT CAME AS A big revelation to me that he was one of those big brown pieces of tin lying out in the pasture only when he stood up and started walking away. I cocked the hammer and put the bead on his shoulder at less than forty yards and when I touched the trigger I saw the hair fly. But it didn't knock him down and he only whirled and started running up the hill. I ran with him, sideways, breaking open the gun and fumbling another shell from my pocket and loading it and shutting it and cocking it again and trying to track him. I couldn't believe it hadn't blown him down. How petrified with fear had they been when he came? At the creep feeder on top of the hill he whirled again, still looking for where the shots were coming from, and it was like he couldn't see me at all, and I leveled on him and fired again, and I knew it was a load of OO buckshot, and a blast seemed to fan around him, some shock wave that hit him but still didn't topple him, and he left running, tail out, streaking low, and I tried to reload again, but it was no use, because he was too fast, and he was headed right toward the cows, standing down there in the bottom below the house, as if he knew somehow that I wouldn't shoot that way, and he dove among them and exited very fast stage left, ducked into the overhanging creek trees, was gone.

I stood there looking after the last fleeting image of him, brown, low to the ground and laid out, getting away. Holding the gun like nothing. And feeling so helpless and hating it so bad. He was just an animal, but still he got the best of me. He came, he saw, he ate, he left. And there was not one thing I could do to prevent any of it, given the circumstances of my station and my family and cattle matters that were out of my hands. But still, it hurt. It hurt about as bad as anything had in a while. They were just so goddamn cute. If you could have seen them, you would know what I mean.

WE DON'T HAVE any goats now. Nanette got sick and died. I found her. I don't know if Tom ever told his children or not. But I guess when they grow up they might read this and finally know.

I keep one of Nanette's horns in my desk drawer. There is also a picture of her on the promo CD of Blue

Mountain's *Dogs Days*. The horn, hollow and fluted, is a spook, a talisman, a key. I keep it here to remind me of what a man can go through for goats. It reminds me of what is possible in this life in the country, and sometimes what is not.

Shack

MOTION: That's what catches the fox's eye. It's the same for me. That's why I see him first some evenings after I've climbed down from the roof.

He has a run he goes into by the overgrown fence, down below where my neighbor Johnny's horses usually graze. One evening, at almost dark, he came out from the fence bushes and walked halfway to the boat dock and then stopped when he saw me. But there was no wind, and I was standing still, and he either couldn't figure out what I was or couldn't smell me, and he went on across the pasture and about his business, which was probably catching his supper. Snacks of field mice. Maybe sleeping birds for a treeclimber like him.

I like it that the fox is there. I hope he'll stay on with me, and that maybe some more frogs will show up. There's only one left from the forty or so I put in the pond five or six years ago. They were a gift in a cardboard box and some boys had caught them for me with their hands in exchange for a reading at the Clarksdale Public Library one night. They must have all left except for this one, or maybe he hopped his way there from somewhere else and never was in the original bunch.

I saw him just this morning, sitting and blending into the cool mud beneath some ferns below the lip of the bank. I got to within ten feet of him and he didn't jump. He has big round dishes under his eyes.

The fox has seen me, I know. He's heard me hammering, and he's probably heard Cher's new song on my radio, and at night when I run the generator and the halogen lights, he's seen and heard all that, too. There are deer that come across the place, that hang around there and drink from the pond. Shane saw one walk across the shallow end, and yesterday I found a bed where one had lain, and their little heartprint hooves have left their signatures in the dry dust of the barn, close to the half-gone salt block. There are a few squirrels, and sometimes a big pileated woodpecker, what the old folks I was raised around called an Indian hen. Once in a while a great gray crane comes to visit and walk in the shallows with his long and bending joints.

FOR A LONG TIME it lies buried in the brain like a seed: a vague idea of a little place somewhere off to itself, four walls to get inside, a roof to keep you from the rain, but where you can sit and watch it come down.

Money and time are problems even if you have the lo-
cation. But there was never any question in my mind
about that. It would be somewhere beside the pond at
Tula, close enough to step out the door and fish. When
I bought eight acres with a house and the pond and a
barn, years back, the house was old, and in a bad state of
disrepair. When I was younger I had known the nice old
lady who lived there. I did some work on it, built a new
front porch, even painted the whole outside, but then
the foundation started sagging because of termites, and
instead of trying to put in a new foundation I had the
house torn down. Even now I'm still chipping the mortar from the chimney bricks in an attempt to salvage
enough of them for maybe a small patio at the shack.
The bricks are handmade and irregular, and I think, old,
maybe very old. Only the bricks and a big silver maple
mark the spot where the house stood for so long, from
before the time when I was a boy and used to open the
gate beside Miss Lutee's house to go down to the pond
and fish. She lived there for a long time, long years ago.

The land slopes down from the road, open pasture except for a few very big sweet gums and catalpas, and on
the back side there are dense stands of old pines, some
cedar and sweet gum, not nearly as many hardwoods as
I'd like, things like red oaks and white oaks and pin
oaks. But eventually there will be a good hardwood forest there. Not in my time, probably, because they grow

so slowly, but maybe my grandchildren will be able to enjoy going over there to fish, and maybe hunting squirrels in the trees that will be grown by then. The little trees are already there, planted by nature, and you can see them if you walk slowly and identify them by their leaves and bark. I'm going to flag the ones I want to keep with surveyor's tape. But the ground is also choked with young sweet gum trees, and they've all got to go, by spray rig and rotary cutter, meaning I have to get the tractor in there eventually, but for now I don't have a road into it. I'm working on that, too, cutting tangles of dead pines killed by the Southern pine beetle, piling wood as I go, spraying and cutting the undergrowth that's left, trying to take back a little bit more each year.

These things take time for one man. Shane's helped me a good bit, though. He's torn down some old fences for me, pulled up the posts and piled wood for me.

Finding the spot was what clinched it for me. Seeing where the house could sit made me start putting it there. But it wasn't an easy place to visualize for a long time. M.A. had pointed to the spot before, had said it would make a good place for a little house. There are two huge pine trees, really big ones that soar on up there. One pretty good-sized cedar is back behind them, and a few elms are scattered to the left side and back, four or five of them. It's a shady spot. It was overrun with briars and honeysuckle and poison ivy and sumac and all kinds of tough slick vines and dead fallen pine trees. The ground rises sharply behind the big pines. It was a mess. But I saw that the trees had grown in such a fashion that a small house might sit right in the middle of them. I took my steel tape back the next time and made a few measurements, stumbling around in the overgrowth and vines, trying to see what might fit in there. And then maybe through grace or something I began to see it. The house could sit back of the two big pines and the left side of it could nestle up pretty close to the tall cedar. Maybe the cedar could be right at the edge of the porch.

The house could sit within a couple of feet of the elms in the back. If the house was small enough it could. A small house, then. Maybe even a tiny house. That way I wouldn't have to cut down any trees. That way I could make the house fit the land. I kind of began to see it. I kind of began to have a vision. That was last summer.

THE TINY BOOK OF TINY HOUSES by Lester Walker is a book I've looked through a lot of times. It has all kinds of interesting houses that people have built through the years, all over the country, and the main thing they all have in common is that they're small. But a small house also means smaller cost. I was thinking about trying somehow to build mine myself. I didn't know how I was going to do it, only that I wanted to, that the actual occupying of it after the building part of it was over would be a constant source of pleasure, to be able to sit in it and remember nailing all of it together.

But everything had to be level and square, didn't it? Everything had to be laid out properly, didn't it? You had to kind of know what you were doing, didn't you? It needed not to leak. It needed to be able to be heated in the winter, maybe cooled a little in the summer. Would it have electricity or would it not? Would it matter? It might. If I was going to write over there I'd need my electric typewriter for sure. I'd need some kick-ass music and there wasn't any doubt about that. On a cool evening in October when turned-orange sycamore leaves were drifting down onto the still face of the pond I might want to plug one of the guitars into the amp and turn it up to Scream to celebrate sundown.

What would it be made of, wood, brick, siding, logs, were log homes hard to build? What if you spent a bunch of money and did it wrong and the roof leaked or none of the windows would open, what would you do then? Just leave it? You'd have to make it right, whatever it took. But is the ordinary person capable of that?

I figured I could get whatever information I needed from books, since there are books about everything, including carpentry, and I had one, and I started looking through it pretty carefully, too. That book was a gift from M.A. a long time back, *Modern Carpentry* by Willis H. Wagner. It showed how to build any damn thing. There were diagrams of how to lay it out, dig the footing, put in the foundation, lay out the walls, raise them, put the roof on, the siding on, the windows and doors in, everything. But it didn't have any tiny houses in it. Still, I figured the same rules of construction would apply for even a small house. So I went back to looking through the other book, the one by Mr. Walker. There was one house in there that had caught my eye in particular.

An architect had built himself a tiny cabin using rough-edged boards for the outside and a steeply pitched roof with an overhang on the front, and three big windows. I loved his roof design but I didn't think I could pull that off. What I was mainly interested in was figuring out how he'd framed it.

I could see that little house, or at least one that vaguely resembled it, sitting up there behind the pond, in the middle of those trees.

I studied the drawings of the construction so closely that sometimes I had to use a magnifying glass to look at the tiniest details. I went over and over the drawings, trying to figure out his floor plan, which was framed up from two twelve-foot beams that were *cantilevered*. I knew that meant something. I had a terrible time trying to figure it out. I'd get back to work and forget about the little house for a while, and then pick up the books again, at night, over coffee, and I began to sketch plans of my own on graph paper so that they would be precise and neat. They were never big houses. I drew different roof plans, drew windows into walls, drew floor plans that showed where things went: a desk, a chair, a stereo. Some even had lofts. A two-story tiny house. In another book I saw one that was indeed split-level, at only six hundred square feet.

The beauty of building a tiny house was that smaller cost, and there would be the intense pleasure of making it, of laying it out with strings and a level. I knew enough to know that you had to drive batter boards in the ground, and use stakes, but I didn't know all the details. I wondered if I might be able to build a floor frame that was sitting on concrete blocks. But the ground was steep for such a short distance. I would have to fit it into the side of that hill.

So I daydreamed some more and drew more plans. I drew trees in the yard and stuff, a puff of smoke from the chimney it might have if I wanted to get elaborate and hire a bricklayer like Gayle Allen, a guy I used to work for. I just wanted to have a little house sitting on that pond.

I spent a lot more time looking through the tiny house book and the carpenter book. I read about cedar shingles, and casement windows, and the different ways you could build a roof, all the interesting things you could do with beams. (Whoa, now. Don't get carried too far away.) I thought of what kind of windows I'd like to have, whether or not it would have a porch (it would, naturally, and possibly a side porch or deck, too), what would the ceiling be like, would it be flat or would it be vaulted, maybe steeply pitched? Beams exposed? Would that be possible? Probably so. Could it have all glass across the front like the architect's little house up in the Adirondacks? If I built it that way it could. There were all kinds of possibilities. I'd looked at pictures of the work done by Frank Lloyd Wright and had admired it for years. I knew that Falling Rock? Falling Water? was cantilevered somehow, maybe long concrete beams laid out to hold a house jutting out on the end? Was that how he'd done it? He figured out how to do just about anything with a building. And this was only going to be a small one. I was probably only limited by my imagination, and the strength of my arms and hands, in what I was physically able to do as far as raising a building by myself went. A building within limits. A building that wouldn't kill me to build it.

I daydreamed more. I wouldn't mention it so much if it hadn't gone on for so long. I kept drawing small houses. Some of them got pretty fancy, lots of nights with the tongue stuck out the corner of the mouth while struggling with a ruler and freshly sharpened pencil as the coffee got cold in the cup. That part of it went on for a long time. But I had to keep making some money, so it took a while before I ever moved the first shovelful of dirt. I sat down for a long time and made some money since there was lots of stuff I needed, lots of stuff indeed. I made a list. I needed wood, nails, maybe concrete blocks. Studs and shingles. I probably needed a new level. I probably needed a new circular saw, hell, the old didn't cut too good anymore. I had a good leather nail apron. But as yet I didn't have a house plan.

I stayed up far later than I should have at night, drinking coffees and more coffees, keeping my pencils short, drawing little houses with my graph paper on my lap while the television played, while books I meant to read went unread and finally back into the dust of the shelves.

I had another book I'd ordered from *Progressive Farmer* magazine a few years back. They happen to have an excellent line of how-to books covering just about any aspect of farm or ranch construction, and this book told in a really simple way how to lay out a house. It was just a matter of establishing the corners with stakes and strings and then making sure the corners were square by measuring with a steel tape across the diagonals. You had little saw kerfs cut into batter boards at the corners and you moved the strings until it was

square. Then you marked your footing and started digging it. But I didn't think I was going to need a footing.
I could see that lots of the houses in Mr. Walker's book
were on simple concrete blocks. That looked like what
I might want to do. A plan began to form in my head.
But it was deadly hot outside. It was August. I decided
to go ahead anyway.

I attacked it first with the chainsaw. Lots of little
bushes and stuff were growing on it. There was poison
ivy all over it, so I had to mix up some 2,4-D and spray
it after I got most of it cut. Ticks kept getting all over
me. But I was carving an enclave out of the wilderness.

After a couple of days of that whacking and cutting,
and being covered with insect bites, it was looking fairly
clear. I was ready to start putting down the frame for the
floor.

In my head and on paper I'd figured it: The house
would be ten by twelve, and the floor frame would be
built of treated two-by-eight joists, doubled on the edges,
spaced on eighteen-inch centers, the backs of them
butting into a doubled two-by-twelve treated beam. The
bottom of them, two feet back from the front wall,
would rest on another beam. Both beams would be sup-
ported by concrete blocks set into the ground or on top
of it, depending on what it took to get it level. I had finally come to understand what *cantilever* meant. In my
case it meant the front two feet of my little house could

project out into thin air because of the beam the floor was resting on. All I had to do was just get the frame square and level. I knew that was going to take a lot of work, but I thought I could do it.

The first day I didn't last long swinging with the pick ax in the hard gray clay. It was like soft rock. And the mosquitoes were feeding on me, and it was noon or near one or something like that, and it just burnt me down. I collapsed with my clothes soaking into the little brown pickup I still had then, and went on home to cool up under the air conditioner. I'd gotten too soft. I hadn't done a decent day's work in years. I knew I just needed to get acclimated.

So I started taking little short trips over. Dig a little, rest a little. I had some strings and stakes and stuff up by then. I could see how far down I needed to dig. The two at the back were just cap blocks, solid concrete four inches thick, but they had to be level with each other. There were tree roots and stuff to deal with. But I felt like I was making progress.

I had to get a board twelve feet long to lay on top of the two blocks so that I could put my level on it and see if it was level. Four or five times of digging and then setting up the board and putting the level on it and looking at it, it wasn't. Then I'd dig some more, go through the whole thing until finally it was.

I had made a run for wood. I had made such a run for

wood that my little truck had gone down the Highway
6 bypass with its nose stuck up toward the sky. I had the
big heavy beams. I had all the two-by-eights it would
take to make all the floor joists. I had brown bags of big
heavy nails. I knew by then how I was going to put the
walls together. And how I was going to raise them. I
was going to use the come-along. Same one I'd pulled
the dead baby calf with so many years back. I knew I
could hitch it to a tree with twenty penny nails and a
log chain, and it would move three tons of whatever
I wanted it to move. I had some frigging *enthusiasm*
built up.

There was indeed one little niggling thing wrong
with my ideal tiny house site. There was a monster
dead pine within about fifty feet of it, and the tree was
easily sixty or seventy feet high. The pine beetles had
killed it. It was far wider through than the bar on my
chain saw, meaning you'd have to attack it from two
sides, the engine screaming, the sawchips flying. It had
been dead long enough for some of the bark to have already fallen off, some of the limbs. And what I should
have done was just suck it up and cut the damn thing
down to start with, as soon as the idea of putting a little
house there began to take on serious consideration in
my brain. But that's not my way usually, to take care of
a potential problem immediately. Oh no. Me, I like to
wait around a good long time and then let things get

serious before I do anything about it. But in all fairness, this tree was a bad son of a bitch. I'm saying this as a semiprofessional ex–pulpwood cutter, a man who's carried a jug of gas and 2-cycle oil around in the woods all day like a goatherder with his sheepgut tankard of old funky hot wine. But a man can get killed real easy messing around with something like cutting down a real big tree and even easier with one like that. So I went happily on with my plans. I didn't cut the tree down. There was nobody to watch above for me for falling limbs while cutting it down, and with a dead one you couldn't ever tell what they were going to do because they didn't react to the cutting of the trunk like a live one did and you never knew what stage of rot the trunk was in unless you'd been watching it. This tree had been dead for a long time. It was just a little worry. It wasn't a big one.

Once in a while, later, after I was underway with construction, I thought about high winds. Or having the little house sitting there and then the tree rotting enough to fall right in the middle of it. But it wasn't a major consideration. Not then.

I nailed the beams together in the carport. I nailed a treated two-by-four ledger all the way across one of them so that the butt ends of the joists could rest on it. That beam would go in the back, between the two solid cap blocks I'd finally gotten level with each other.

It was hotter than the hind wheels of hell. You'd swing the hammer for a few minutes and the sweat would start coming through your shirt. If you kept on, your hair would turn into a crown of sweat and even your pants would stick to your legs. I figured as long as I didn't make myself fall out with a stroke I'd be okay. Hell, I was damn near fifty.

All that stuff was heavy, heavy, heavy. I have to carry every piece of lumber across the spillway of my pond and up the hill about fifty or sixty feet to the little house. That's after I back all the way across the levee because there's not enough room to turn around at the end. That treated lumber has a lot of moisture in it because of the stuff they pump into it to make it impervious to rot and termites for forty years. That's with direct ground contact. That's what they say. We'll see. It's supposed to have a money-back guarantee.

I had the other blocks. They were hollow, but I was going to fill them with concrete. This is how I laid it out: I had stakes driven that outlined a twelve-by-ten-foot rectangle. Four stakes. I tied a piece of twine from the back stake on each side to the front stake on each side, and then I hung a little thing called a line level on it. It costs about four bucks. It's a little plastic tube with an oil-filled bubble inside it, with little hooks to hang it on a line. It works just like a carpenter's level. I adjusted the string on the back stake so that it was resting level on the block, and then I pulled it on out and tied it to a front stake. I read the level and drove the front stake a little deeper, carefully. Once I got it level, I could measure with my tape down from the bottom of the string and add the width of the beam and the thickness of the concrete block to tell me how far down into the ground I needed to dig to make the house level against the hill it was going to be sitting on. It turned out to be about five inches. I dug it, sweating in September's heat by then, the boys already out with their guns for doves, people already reconnoitering the woods with their four-wheelers on the back ends of their trucks. Orange vests would be out soon, all the pickups in the roads with the guns in the rack. I ran another string between the two front stakes and got that one level, too. Level all four ways. I was set after that.

I dug, I set the blocks. I cut my joists in the carport and made sure that everything was going to fit together. I had old sawhorses that fell apart and I went out to Wal-Mart for new ones that you just clamped together on some two-by-fours you'd cut, and they didn't work worth a shit. One leg was always falling or something while you had the saw running. I cussed and fussed. But finally I had it all ready.

A groove was coming. The weather was cooling and I had money in the bank from the work I'd done. I had to go teach in Montana the next year, sure, but that was no big deal. I figured I'd probably have my book finished by then. The important thing was to get as much work done on this thing as I could now, while the weather was cool, while I had the money to buy the material, the time to do it. Maybe maybe maybe get the roof on before winter rains set in. Because when they set in here, they set in.

The truth is that if I hadn't gotten sober for a long time the year before, none of it would have happened. The idea of building it had always been in my head. It had probably been in my head for ten years. I work hard, and I play too hard all the time. But I get sober for a while, and I look around, and I see what all is possible. It's always a revelation. I saw that I felt good enough to do the physical labor that would be required, and be able to put in the hours it would take. I might not do it all at once, probably wouldn't, because there would be other things that would come up that I'd have to do, but when those times came along I could just wait. Bide my time.

In two afternoons I nailed the frame together, on site. I ran my steel tape from corner to corner and bumped it this way or that until I had it square. I doublechecked it twice. It looked good to me, and I started nailing the subflooring on. It was three-quarter-inch sheets of four-by-eight flakeboard. In almost no time at all there was a nice level square platform of new wood twelve by ten sitting in that little glade I had chosen for myself.

It's hard to say what it felt like. It felt more than good. I carried my guitar over there a few times late in the evenings and just sat there and played it, listening to the last of the crickets. Before long they wouldn't be singing at all. And the frog would be sleeping some-where deep in the mud.

The squirrels would still be around. The hordes of hunters would be after the deer. They'd probably get all jumpy and nervous. I would be too if somebody was af-ter my ass with a gun all the time. I wanted to go on and work on it, start putting the walls up. But then I had to do a bunch of other stuff I didn't want to do. But it was stuff that had to be done.

SOME PEOPLE THINK a writer can't drive a nail. Look at Thoreau and you know that's bullshit. He built that whole thing on the pond for about fifteen bucks.

I had to paint the house we live in. All the outside doors. There are eight of them. Two of them are double doors. You have to inch very slowly and carefully along the gaskets of the doors with the edge of your paint-brush, dipping frequently, that is, if you are a fastidious painter, which I believe I am. I feel there can be no other kind. Some people want to just slop shit all over another

door or something. But that's not my way. I like to be
careful with the stuff that belongs to me.

I had to paint the whole underside of my front porch,
which is sixty feet long. I had to spray all the mildew off
the underside of my carport, which is about twenty by
thirty-five. I had to build five new posts for my front
porch out of clear pine one-by-sixes and I had to set up
the sawhorses and wear an apron all day long and make
sandwiches for myself while everybody was gone. It
went on and on. It got ridiculous. I was even painting
outside at night sometimes wearing a black leather
jacket. I got some blue paint on it. It's still on it.

It went on from about the twenty-second of September until the fourth of November. In between all that I
cooked a chicken stew for two hundred people, sat
around some campfires with friends, played some guitars, cleaned out my old writing room and repainted it
and moved back into it, read a bunch of books, got rid of
a car and bought another one, did some driving around,
and tried to learn a few new chords.

I finally got through with all that stuff and went and
bought studs, long two-by-fours for the top plates, long
treated two-by-fours for the sole plates. After months
of studying the pages of *Modern Carpentry*, I knew
again what a header was and how to build one, had re-
acquainted myself with the process of building a corner or a tee. When I was a lot younger I had worked for

David Parker, putting in additions and doing carpenter work on jobs like that, but I hadn't learned anything, had only nailed where they told me to, and in truth hadn't wanted to learn any of it, was only earning a paycheck while I was getting ready to get married and live a life of happy harmony with my new wife.

Now I began to see why things were done the way they were, that there was a reason for everything in carpentry. I decided to raise the east wall first. It was on the short, ten-foot side, and it only had one window in it. And I already had all my windows, and a door with fifteen panes, and a generator, all bought out of the Home Depot on I-55 up near Hernando where my little brother lives. I'd done a lot of studying about windows and I'd decided that I wanted three across the front, just like the little architect's cabin, but with one on the east side, and I figured that I wanted them about three feet wide, or a little less, and about four feet high, two panes that swung outward with hand cranks. I knew they'd be high-dollar, but it just so happened that on the Sunday afternoon we went to Home Depot to look about windows and a door, we found four that were exactly what I wanted that somebody had ordered and then failed to pick up. They were three hundred dollars apiece. Twelve hundred dollars worth of windows. But the dude with the orange apron said he'd check and see what they'd take and came back in a few minutes and said I could get them all for six hundred. I loaded them up on the cart, found a door for $115 and put it on the cart, found a gasoline generator for $400 and put it on the cart, and we strapped all that stuff into the back end of Billy Ray's pickup and brought it home. So I knew what size my window openings had to be.

I screwed up some things, I know that. You have to screw up a few things to ever learn anything about what you're doing. That probably goes for brain surgery or shoeing a horse. It probably goes for making love or preaching, for war or meditation, for any of the things you don't yet know how to do very well.

I framed up the east wall and built the header for it correctly and was able to raise it by myself and secure it temporarily with some loose studs nailed to standing studs and the elms outside that wall. I took a picture of it. I'd been taking pictures of it since the first day, when there was only one board on the ground. I was kind of documenting the thing as I went along.

The south wall went up next, but I had a special plan for it. It was going to have three small windows, maybe ten inches high and less than two feet long, and they wouldn't be windows that would open. They would just be panes of glass sealed into the wall to admit a little light. But each one of them would have a piece of art work etched into it in acid, a piece of work done by each of my children, and they would go in descending order from east to west across the back wall, the tallest one for Billy Ray, the second one for Shane, and the last one for LeAnne. I figured, maybe incorrectly, that each would need its own header, and it took me a long time to build that wall. It was twelve feet long. I had to make sure my measurements were exact, and that old carpenter thing kept going through my head: Measure twice, cut once.

I kept the radio going, tunes blasting out onto the quiet of the pond. I carried my lunch or went up to the store for sandwiches and pints of milk and little bags of potato chips. I could stretch out in the shade after a big lunch, after eating a dill pickle. They were good days. But when I finally got the damn thing built it was way too heavy for me to lift. So many headers had put the weight on it.

I prized it up off the floor with a crowbar enough to slide a piece of wood under the top plate. Then I prized it up high enough to stick a brick under it. And then I prized it up enough to stick a concrete block up under it. I had her ass then.

I went around to one of the big pines in the front and picked up the log chain and my hammer and some extra big nails and tacked that chain in a loop around the trunk. Then I made a loop in the chain with the hook and picked up the hook of my come-along and set it in it.

How the hell did some dude, back in France five hundred years ago, pick up some two-ton stone to cap off a cathedral that was ten stories high? I was just trying to raise a little stud wall.

Once I stretched the cable out, all I had to do was wrap it around the top plate and go back to the handle, to ratchet it back and forth. I took a picture of that, too, the chain tight as Dick's hatband coming off the tree and the wall halfway up. I toenailed short pieces of two-by-four at the sole plate to keep it from skidding across the floor and make it rise up. I had built the corners into each of the two walls so that I could lock the first corner together with nails once I had it up. It was still hot. The crickets were always singing in the trees. The station from Tupelo always sold cars and talked about restaurants over there. They sold the hell out of mobile homes. They played the same songs everybody all over America heard. But the radio was also easy to listen to. You just stuck some batteries in it and you could even leave it out in the rain if you wanted to. It didn't matter. I could always buy another one. The fox could listen to it while I was gone.

It took some lifting and shoving around and some very careful maneuvering to get the south wall in place. It was so heavy I couldn't risk it falling on me. As soon as I could I braced it upright with some loose two-by-fours. By loosening things and renailing things and hitting things with a hammer I was able to bring it into position and then by a great stroke of good luck, working by myself like that, bring it into alignment with the corner I'd built into the east wall, finally making a solid corner—two walls of studs that could stand by themselves. Maybe.

I felt like it was a lot to get done. It looked good. I knew I'd have to raise the north wall next, since it would be hardest, because it had all three of those windows in it, but I wanted to get the hard part out of the way and then frame the last wall with the door and put it all up and have four walls standing. Then seal all the corners together with the doubled top plate. Then get ready to cut some rafters. It was warming up into October. I heard gunshots. The days were getting shorter and shorter. And the time was shorter than I knew. I didn't know that rain was coming. And as soon as I finished this wallframing, M.A. suffered an attack of the gall bladder and had to be hospitalized, and operated on for it, and I had to stop what I was doing and go through that with her. It's very clear how it happened, according to my daily journal:

> *November 6, 1998*
> Went to Tula soon as
> I could & started
> laying out the north

wall, got one 12 inch
header in & worked till dark, went
home & got ready to
take M.A. to Ajax.
Ate, came home & played
till M.A. started yelling
for B.R. around two A.M. Got
her up & dressed & took
her to the hospital,
they admitted her, kept
her knocked out with
November 7
Demerol most of the
day. She had a bad
time all day long,
cried & suffered and
slept by turns.
Slept when I could and went home for a
little while & came back, slept on
couch in 3rd Floor
Lobby.
November 8
Operated on her at
9:30, took out her
gall bladder, brought
her back about 1:30.
Stayed with her,

slept on the couch
again, got very
little sleep.
She got pissed off because
me and Billy Ray were
telling jokes and
laughing in her room.

I started back to work on the north wall a few days after I got her home. Oh she was sick. Laid up in the hospital before they operated on her Billy Ray and I both
held up blue plastic hospital bowls for her to puke this
old yellow stuff in. Gall, I guess it was. I guess she had
a bladder full of that old stuff.

On the sixteenth of November, one sunny afternoon
when she was feeling better, I hauled her over there and
hauled her a chaise longue over there and got her up the
hill so she could be close to where I was working and
started framing up the north wall, the one that would
have the three big windows in it. She lay there all afternoon and watched me cut and build up the other two
headers just like the first one, all of them three inches
too short exactly. Just from me not paying enough attention to what I was doing. There wasn't anything to
do but throw them away and get some more material
and start all over again. But I didn't have time to do all
that in one afternoon. I hauled her home and waited.

THOSE DAYS CAME, when I was free to hammer and saw as much as I wanted to. Nobody was messing with me. There was still money in the bank. I started over on the north wall and this time I remembered to include that one-and-a-half-inch stud thickness on each side of the headers when I was building them. The windows were so wide that I had to move them pretty close together to get all three of them in the front wall. But that was the way I wanted it: a wall of mostly unbroken glass across the front, where I could sit at my desk and look out the window at the pond, in snow or rain, in dawn's first weak light or the shadows of evening. I damn near got killed getting that one up.

It took a while to build it. I was trying to be careful, and moving all the windows so close together meant the wall needed more studs somehow, more than the south wall had. All three of the headers in the north wall were built up out of two-by-twelves. It was real heavy. But smart me just did the same thing he did on the back wall, hooked it up to the old come-along and started winching that baby up. Too bad I didn't think to put something out front to stop it from falling the other way. But you live and learn. Sometimes it seems to me like I live and don't learn anything. As heavy as that thing was, I should have known that I wouldn't be able to keep it balanced long enough to slide it over and nail it into the east wall. But I got it up, by stages, and when

I went to slide it over toward the east wall, it occurred to me that I hadn't nailed any short two-by-fours on the corner studs to keep it from falling off the floor. And about that time it leaned a little too far toward the pond, and I couldn't catch it, and tried to, and at the last moment I saw that we were going to crash out front against the big pine tree, and the only thing I could do in a split second of self-preservation was climb up into the middle window opening and ride it into the cedar tree, thence into the pines. It all happened pretty fast and I knew after we settled that I'd hurt my leg pretty bad. It was hurting so bad I was scared to look at it. The amazing thing was that it didn't hurt the wall. It only fell about three feet but I got slammed. That's what Shane would say. I hobbled around and cried for a little bit because my leg was hurting so bad and then I finally got up my guts and raised my right jeans leg and there was a very deep puncture wound in my shinbone or at least the muscle that covered it. I hobbled around some more, smoked a cigarette, cussed a little. I rested some, mopping at the sweat. Before the sun went down I had started dragging the north wall back up into position. You can't let a bunch of wood just beat you.

THE DAY CAME when I sat on top of the four walls and nailed the top plates down, locking all the corners together. I plumbed the corners with a carpenter's level and nailed them into place with braces. But the days had flown. The ground around my feet was littered with falling leaves. There was no time to sit inside the walls and play the guitar. Rafters had to go up soon, and then the decking, and then whatever would cover them and keep the rain out.

My problem was that I didn't know how to cut a rafter. It was all explained in the carpentry book, but somehow I just couldn't get it. There was pitch, so much drop in a running foot, varying degrees of it. And how was I going to raise the ridgepole by myself and hold it in place long enough to nail the rafters on? I couldn't be in two places on a twelve-foot span at once.

It was a problem. I just had to figure it out. And at this point, standing on top of the plate, we're talking not about falling three feet but eleven feet.

I went to the building supply and bought the straightest fourteen-foot, two-by-six spruce I could find. I bought a number of eight-foot-long two-by-sixes for rafters. I had to make something to help myself. I had to make some more hands. Shane was in school, college. Billy Ray was working, rolling his combine through fields of soybeans seven days a week, from dawn till dark and beyond. One afternoon I went and rode with him, up high in the seat of the big green John Deere, the

wide-turning blades of the header bringing in six rows
of beans at once. Deer stood at the edges of fields and
chewed and watched. Rabbits scattered everywhere.

I knew the principles of a plumb bob. It was nothing
but another form of the level. What I figured to do was
build a frame of something somehow on each side of the
house, something that was about three feet high, something with a slot in it that would let me rest each end
of the fourteen-foot spruce in it, then get up over it,
hang a plumb bob over it, and then rock it back and
forth until I had it dead center over a mark I'd be putting
on the top plates of the east and and west walls that was
dead center lengthwise on them, and then nail it in
place.

It was hell to do and took a long time but I got it done
and it worked. But with the ridgepole stuck out on the
end I could mark the first rafter, making a simple plumb
cut on the top, then notching it into the top plate by
marking it with a pencil and cutting it. After that first
one I had a pattern. I cut all the rest of them the same
way. If I'd done right, they'd fit.

Shane was home on the twenty-fifth of November,
the day before Thanksgiving, and we put them all on in
one day. I watched him nail the rafters onto the ridge of
the little house, and his steps were sure on the joists he
was standing on, actually beams I'd formed up out of
tripled two-by-sixes that would be exposed in the ceil-

ing when the house was finished, and his stroke with the hammer was steady and hard. He's a natural car-penter, something I have to work hard at to achieve any-thing resembling level or square. He would hold some nails in his mouth while he was hammering, and we nailed on all the rafters that afternoon.

In one day I put all the decking on. It was tough, working off a ladder and then climbing up and nailing it down, and making sure it all fit right, and already rain was drifting in and telling me to hurry. I hurried and I hurried, but I didn't make it.

Again there was other stuff to do. The things of life. I needed to get back to real work. The house needed some shingles on it. After all that work and new wood, it needed to be protected from the rain. But those deck-ing nails were the last nails I drove into it that year. It sat there in the winter and the rain came down, leaking between the cracks in the decking, dripping down onto the new floor, where it would puddle in spots of saw-dust. A chill wind held it in its grip. The old dead pine sat there, never swaying in the wind. And the fox must have had a warm place where he hid. There was no warm place in my little house for sure. Unless maybe he got up under it and slept there, in the dead grass and dry leaves the floor had covered.

✦ ✦ ✦

THE FOLLOWING SUMMER I bought Western red cedar shingles imported from British Columbia at $219 per square, hefty when you realize that asphalt ones run about thirty. But they were what I wanted and I put them on. Each is somewhere between four and fourteen inches wide, twenty-four inches long, thick at one end, thin at the other. You have to overlap each one with its brothers below to make sure water doesn't run in between the gaps. It took a long time, working off a scaffold, climbing up and down, throwing more shingles up, getting on and off.

My little roof is pretty steep. You can slide your ass right off if you aren't careful. But I figured that would just help it shed the rainwater better. I'd read all about the shingles in the carpentry book. I knew they'd look great, too. It took me weeks and weeks to get them on. It got so hot in the daytime that I went to working at night, setting up the lights with the generator, and then the bugs came in so thick you could hardly see how to nail. But that's just summer. That's just a part of the life we have here.

I built the ridgecap from a fourteen-foot piece of zinc that was fourteen inches wide. I nailed it down and swept off the splinters and loose nails and climbed down.

I was scared to do it, but I cut the big tree down, safely, breaking it into two huge pieces against a tremendous post oak at Cordis Foster's fenceline. Then it was time to go to Montana. It was August again. And I did go, and now am back again here, and the little house sits windowless but roofed, a few pieces of siding on it now where Billy Ray and Shane helped me one of the last evenings I was here last year. I've still got to get those windows in, build the cornices, hang the door, build the decks and finish all the outside, then the inside. It'll be years at this rate. But it's okay. It's something to keep looking forward to. One day, maybe I will eventually sit in it and either write something on a piece of paper or play a few chords on a guitar.

I go over there all the time. I look across the pond at it when I drive up. In the summer you can barely see it. I like that. I go and sit in it if I know a rain storm is coming. It does not leak.